# MTEL®

# Music

## Practice Questions

I0802517



Mometrix
TEST PREPARATION

# DEAR FUTURE EXAM SUCCESS STORY

First of all, **THANK YOU** for purchasing Mometrix study materials!

Second, congratulations! You are one of the few determined test-takers who are committed to doing whatever it takes to excel on your exam. **You have come to the right place.** We developed these practice tests with one goal in mind: to deliver you the best possible approximation of the questions you will see on test day.

Standardized testing is one of the biggest obstacles on your road to success, which only increases the importance of doing well in the high-pressure, high-stakes environment of test day. Your results on this test could have a significant impact on your future, and these practice tests will give you the repetitions you need to build your familiarity and confidence with the test content and format to help you achieve your full potential on test day.

**Your success is our success**

**We would love to hear from you!** If you would like to share the story of your exam success or if you have any questions or comments in regard to our products, please contact us at **800-673-8175** or **support@mometrix.com**.

Thanks again for your business and we wish you continued success!

Sincerely,
The Mometrix Test Preparation Team


Printed in the United States of America

# Table of Contents

# Practice Test #1

**1. Which of the following practice techniques is most important for beginning instrumentalists when they practice on their own at home?**

a. Many short sessions
b. Breaking music apart
c. Establishing a routine
d. Self-regulated learning

**2. Which of the following regions of the world does the gamelan come from?**

a. Pakistan
b. Indonesia
c. China
d. Australia

**3. Which of the following musical terms most closely means "to perform at your pleasure" and without a strict tempo, as in a cadenza?**

a. A Niente
b. A Battuta
c. A Piacere
d. A Cappella

**4. A wind ensemble performs a piece in sonata form. How do they achieve beatless sonority when modulating?**

a. Instruments performing the fundamental tones use a tuner to play with equal-tempered tuning, and other instruments compromise with embouchure adjustments and alternate fingerings to play with just intonation throughout the key changes.
b. Performers take into account that the equal-tempered tuning system is a compromise and that certain pitches and harmonies will naturally be slightly out-of-tune through key changes.
c. All instruments play with equal-tempered tuning in order to end the movement or piece on the same reference pitch within the key that the piece began.
d. Adjust the entire ensemble's reference pitches to equal temperament throughout the exposition, development, and recapitulation.

**5. In which of the following music careers does a person work with a record label to scout and sign talent for recording contracts?**

a. Artists and repertoire (A&R) representative
b. Licensing administrator
c. Agent
d. Artist manager

**6. Compared to other leaders in music education, which of the following theories about learning is most related to Orff Schulwerk?**

a. Music is a language
b. Ontologic follows phylogenic
c. There must be a systematic method
d. Teaching must be based on Piaget's model of child development

**7. Which of the following adjustments should trumpet players most attend to when first learning how to play higher notes?**

a. Lifting the tongue and reducing volume of air
b. Lowering the tongue and increasing the volume of air
c. Tightening the aperture and creating more diaphragm pressure
d. Strengthening the embouchure to handle the increased amount of air

**8. Which of the following composers wrote an opera based upon Shakespeare's *Othello*?**

a. Verdi
b. Puccini
c. Berlioz
d. Handel

**9. What is the name of the note below?**

a. Hemidemisemiquaver
b. Demisemiquaver
c. Semiquaver
d. Quaver

**10. The music excerpt below is an example of which of the following subgenres of early 20th century classical music?**

a. Serialist
b. Minimalist
c. Romantic
d. Neoclassical

**11. Which of the following major approaches to music education is this basic lesson process most reflective of?**

> Over the course of several class periods, an elementary school music teacher tells a story about life in a South American village, including musical customs related to heritage, the ambient sounds of the community, surrounding geography, and indigenous wildlife. The teacher plays audio recordings, shows pictures and videos, and then asks the students to imagine and talk about the music, movement, and sounds that they might hear while living in this area.
> The lesson process continues as students use created and classroom instruments, along with their bodies and voices, to replicate what they might experience, creating a soundscape to be performed during the retelling of the story.
> The teacher then teaches the students a related, authentic folk song.

Finally, the teacher directs the class to create a composition, using real or made-up symbols and notation, to accompany a poem that is inserted into the middle of the folk song. Students also choreograph pantomime, movement, and dance, along with body percussion and vocal sounds to enrich the composition. Students are directed to create space for improvising with the mediums within their composition. This composition is written on big chart paper for the class to follow. The class is divided into sections and performs each part of this composition. Students are invited to share thoughts, what they have learned, and their imaginings and feelings throughout the process.

a. Gordon
b. Dalcroze
c. Orff
d. Laban

**12. Which of the following is the most appropriate first step to tuning a student-level flute?**

a. Check that the head-joint cork is in the right place using the cleaning rod's tick mark with the center of the embouchure hole.
b. Ensure that the distance from the keys to each hole is adjusted appropriately by the manufacturer.
c. Pull out the head-joint by approximately one-eighth to one-quarter of an inch and tune to a concert A.
d. Roll your flute in and out from your blowing angle to raise or lower the pitch.

**13. Which of the following compositional devices is used in the final measures of the following music excerpt?**

(Chopin *Nocturne Op. 9,* No. 1 in Bb Minor Larghetto)

a. Whole-tone scale
b. Octatonic scale
c. Picardy third
d. Sequence

**14. Which of the following "Mighty Five" compositional techniques is used in the following music excerpt?**

(Mussorgsky, *Pictures at an Exhibition*, "Promenade")

a. Modular rotation
b. Heterophony
c. Whole-tone scale
d. Octatonic scale

**15. What is one reason why ukuleles might be used in general music classrooms instead of guitars?**

a. Guitars are less prone to damage in low humidity
b. Guitars are generally more expensive
c. Guitars are less preferred by students
d. Guitars have a more restricted range of tone

**16. Which of the following harmonic analyses best represents the music excerpt below?**

(J.S. Bach chorale, BWV 104)

a. $I - II^{6/5} - I^{6} - IV - V^{6/4} - V^{7} - vi - I$
b. $I - IV^{6} - I^{6} - V^{7} - I^{6/5} - V^{6/5} - V^{7} - I$
c. $I - I - IV^{6} - V - ii - I^{6} - V - I$
d. $I - I - III - V^{7} - ii - I^{6} - V^{7} - I$

**17. Given the following music excerpt, which of the following saxophone fingerings for Bb is most appropriate for fingering the Bb in the first measure?**

a. 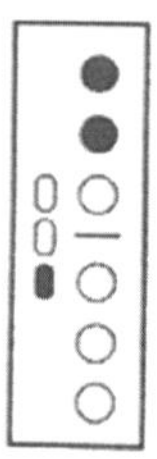

b. 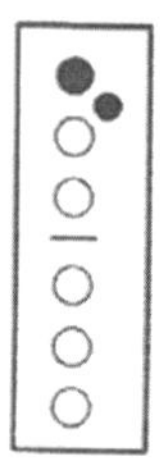

c. 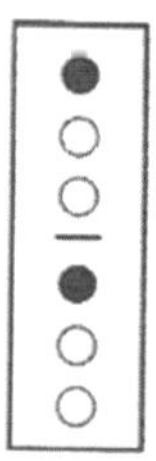

d. 

**18. Which of the following administrative positions is best handled exclusively by an adult without student ensemble member participation?**

a. Librarian to collect and catalogue music
b. Secretary for attendance and note-taking
c. Uniform manager to manage uniform records
d. Treasurer to collect proceeds and maintain records

**19. When teaching trumpet, which of the following is the best time to teach the third valve slide adjustment for intonation?**

a. As soon as possible
b. After two to four years of playing
c. Advanced high school
d. Preparation for college music majors

**20. What is one reason why there is a movement in lower elementary general music classes to replace teaching soprano recorder with ukulele?**

a. The ukulele is an accompanying instrument
b. The ukulele sounds better in a group setting
c. The ukulele is easier to learn than the recorder
d. The ukulele is more culturally relevant in society

**21. New teachers taking over successful music programs should prioritize which of the following behaviors?**

a. Establishing their own protocols to demonstrate that there is new leadership
b. Establishing contact with parents to inform them of a change in the program
c. Establishing contact with the outgoing director to ease the transition
d. Establishing a needed budget for capital and operating expenses

**22. Which of the following purposes of using a student portfolio is most related to a working portfolio?**

a. The working portfolio contains artifacts to showcase to others, such as parents, next year's teacher, or even potential employers.
b. The working portfolio contains artifacts for students and teachers to document student learning or mastery of a concept.
c. The working portfolio contains artifacts that are both complete and incomplete for the student to use for self-diagnosis.
d. The working portfolio contains artifacts completed over an extended period of time to demonstrate student growth.

**23. Which of the following initial techniques used to teach students to sing harmony is most appropriate?**

a. Singing root harmonies
b. Singing in thirds
c. Singing drones in fifths
d. Experimenting to find harmony while someone else sings melody

**24. Which of the following harmonic analyses best represents the music excerpt below?**

**Alle Menschen müssen sterben**

(J.S. Bach chorale, BWV 262)

a. I – $V^6$ – $I^6$ – IV – $I^{6/5}$ – V – III – I
b. I – III – V – VI – ii – $V/V^7$ – I – I
c. I – $II^{6/5}$ – $I^6$ – IV – $V^{6/4}$ – $V^7$ – vi – I
d. I – vi – $I^6$ – IV – V – V – I – I

**25. In a traditional high school music theory class, which of the following sequences of concepts from common practice period is most appropriate to teach?**

a. Dominant seventh chords in root position, the III chord
b. Six-four chords, seventh chords in various inversions
c. Root position part-writing, modulations
d. Secondary dominant chords, enharmonic modulations

**26. When a student memorizes common practice period rules, such as the four uses of the second inversion tonic chord, which of the following parts of Bloom's taxonomy is being most engaged?**

a. Knowledge
b. Comprehension
c. Application
d. Analysis

**27. Which of the following techniques for achieving blend in an alto saxophone section is the most practical factor in getting the section to perform so that there is one homogenous blend of sound?**

a. Have all students play with the same ligature.
b. Have all students play with reeds of similar strength.
c. Have all students play the same brand instrument.
d. Have all students play with similarly constructed mouthpieces.

**28. For beginning clarinet players, which of the following pitches are best used in sequence to help the player tune the instrument to itself and then to an ensemble?**

a. E3, G5
b. G4, G3
c. C4, C5
d. G3, E4

**29. What is the name for the following music symbol?**

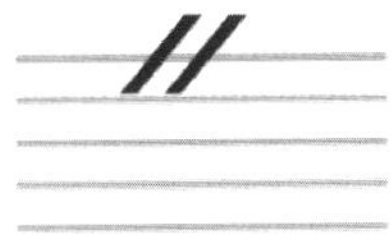

a. Fermata
b. Caesura
c. Crotchet
d. Sesquiflat

**30. Which instrumentalist must be able to read the alto clef?**

a. Oboe
b. Viola
c. Trombone
d. Baritone saxophone

**31. Which of the following is an advantage of using modern, high quality synthetic reeds made of composite materials?**

a. They need to be wet when played
b. They sound the same over time
c. They warp through extended use
d. They sound superior to cane reeds

**32. Which of the following keys is a standard English horn pitched in?**

a. Concert C
b. Concert F
c. Concert Eb
d. Concert Bb

**33. Which of the following ensemble rehearsal pacing shapes is the most appropriate representation for the usual flow of intensity of an ensemble rehearsal?**

a. 

b. 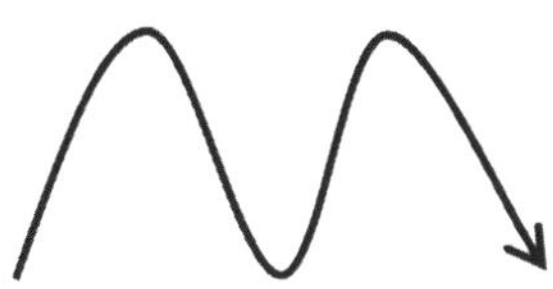

c. 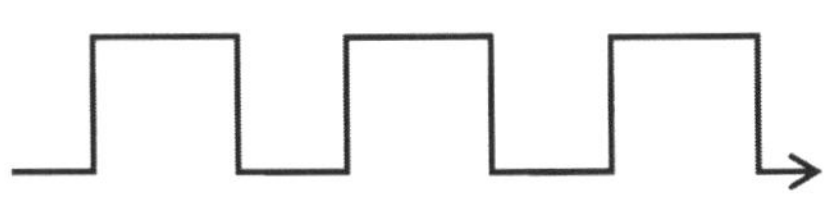

d. 

**34. Which of the following textures in music is characterized by a single melodic line with instrumental accompaniment?**

a. Heterophony
b. Homophony
c. Polyphony
d. Homonymy

**35. Which of the following is generally considered an advantage of a mixer over an audio interface for a recording studio?**

a. Greater portability
b. Less expensive
c. Overall simpler to use
d. More control of sound

**36. Which of the following rationales best justifies a teacher who advocates for beginning trumpet players to use both letter names and tonal syllables when learning songs by rote, by ear, and by notation?**

a. It prevents students from being confused with multiple systems.
b. It makes transposition easier than using note names and steps.
c. It makes the learning of music reading much faster.
d. It makes transfer to other brass instruments easier.

**37. Which of the following types of rating scales is illustrated?**

| <u>**Checklist to Measure Students' Ability to Distinguish and Sing Individual Pitches When Presented with a Major Tonic Chord**</u> |
|---|
| 1. Student responds = 1 point |
| 2. Sings root (*do*) = 1 point |
| 3. Sings fifth (*so*) = 1 point |
| 4. Sings third (*mi*) = 2 points |
| TOTAL POINTS = ________ |

a. Single-dimensional additive rating scale
b. Single-dimensional cumulative rating scale
c. Hybrid multi-dimensional additive rating scale
d. Hybrid single-dimensional cumulative rating scale

**38. Compared to the Classical era, which of the following stylistic characteristics of this music excerpt best exemplifies that it was composed during the Baroque era?**

(Bach's Keyboard Sonata in D minor BWV 964)

a. Basso continuo
b. Polyphonic texture
c. Continuous motion
d. Symmetrical melody

**39. Which of the following composers arranged the piece exemplified by the music excerpt for orchestra?**

a. Hindemith
b. Stravinsky
c. Orff
d. Ravel

**40. Which of the following music characteristics is the most helpful information for determining when the following music excerpt was composed?**

a. Rhythmic modes
b. Three-voice organum
c. Sustained cantus firmus
d. Composed in the *ars nova* style

**41. A high school physics class is presented with the following information and follow-up question:**

- Pitches on music instruments raise when the instrument is warmed up
- Music instruments expand—become larger—when warmed up
- Larger music instruments play lower pitches

**Which of the following explanations about tuning an instrument as it gets warmed up best explains why the pitch rises even though the instrument gets larger?**

a. The instrument becomes used to its ambient surroundings.
b. The instrument gets thicker, making the tone hole smaller.
c. The instrument gravitates to the factory manufacturing specifications.
d. The instrument pitch is raised by the performer's embouchure adjustments.

**42. Which of the following statements about twelve-tone music is most correct?**

a. A note can generally be repeated before the series of other notes have occurred.
b. The order of notes is variable and not fixed throughout the composition.
c. All twelve notes of the chromatic scale must be within the prime row.
d. The prime row cannot be inverted until it is written in retrograde.

**43. When adjusting levels for your microphone through a mixer on digital audio workstation software and an audio interface, which decibels relative to full scale (dBFS) level should your audio recording software peak at?**

a. 0 dBFS
b. −3 dBFS
c. −6 dBFS
d. −12 dBFS

**44. Which of the following jazz standards is performed in the bossa nova style?**

a. "Desafinado"
b. "What Is This Thing Called Love"
c. "Cherokee"
d. "How High the Moon"

**45. Which of the following book series published by GIA helps music teachers seeking the best possible music at all levels, with appropriate analyses and rehearsal and performance practices for each composition?**

a. *Developing the Complete Band Program*
b. *The Creative Director: Alternative Rehearsal Techniques*
c. *Note Grouping: A Method for Achieving Expression and Style in Musical Performance*
d. *Teaching Music Through Performance in Band*

**46. Which of the twelve-tone rows represents the retrograde of the illustrated prime row 0 given below?**

0 – 8 – 9 – 6 – 7 – 3 – 4 – 2 – 5 – 10 – 11 – 1

a. 11 – 1 – 2 – 7 – 10 – 8 – 9 – 5 – 6 – 3 – 4 – 0
b. 0 – 10 – 9 – 4 – 3 – 1 – 2 – 6 – 5 – 8 – 7 – 11
c. 1 – 9 – 10 – 7 – 8 – 4 – 5 – 3 – 6 – 11 – 0 - 2
d. 1 – 11 – 10 – 5 – 2 – 4 – 3 – 7 – 6 – 9 – 8 – 0

**47. Which of the following vocal practices produces tension in the tongue?**

a. Forming consonants with the tongue toward the front of the mouth
b. Dropping the tongue down in the center of the mouth cavity
c. Placing the tip of the tongue behind the bottom teeth
d. Tucking in the chin to position the tongue

**48. Which of the following vocal agility considerations is among the first building blocks when learning to increase quickness and flexibility between notes in melismatic music and the music of Bach and Handel?**

a. Learning to slur notes
b. Increasing tongue and jaw movement
c. Moving as quickly as possible through the scale
d. Incorporating consonants in between open vowels

**49. Which of the following music eras is the following music excerpt likely from?**

a. Baroque
b. Classical
c. Romantic
d. Neoclassical

**50. Which of the following interval pattern sequences does Kodály advocate teaching students to sing?**

a. *So-mi, so-mi-la*
b. *So-mi, mi-re-do*
c. *Mi-re-do, fa-ti*
d. *Mi-re-do, so-mi-la*

**51. Which of the following drum rudiments is characterized by the stick pattern illustrated?**

a. Five-stroke roll
b. Double ratamacue
c. Double paradiddle
d. Flamacue

**52. Which of the following is a beginning tuba player likely to have the LEAST amount of practice with in a traditional ensemble?**

a. Performing melodic parts
b. Playing harmonies
c. Performing bass lines
d. Playing on time

**53. Which of the following physical actions performed on a student best legally defines "physical restraint"?**

a. Personal restriction that prevents a student from moving
b. Physical escort to a school safety officer or front office
c. The use of any device to restrict a student's mobility
d. Vehicle safety apparatus used to transport a student

**54. Which of the following artifacts for a digital assessment portfolio is best suited for grade 1 general music classes?**

a. A photo collage of students participating in music activities throughout the year.
b. A digital drawing of a melodic contour of a song being learned in class.
c. A digital photo of a word cloud of music terms and symbols.
d. A computer screen capture of the cycle of fourths.

**55. Which of the following reasons for administering a standardized timbre preference test is most appropriate for beginning music instrumentalists?**

a. To increase student achievement and retention
b. To help balance the instrumentation within a performance ensemble
c. To help students see beyond physical and social attributes that may influence their choice of instrument
d. To help teachers offer harder-to-learn music instruments to students with higher music aptitudes

**56. When using rating scales, checklists, and holistic rubrics to measure and evaluate individual achievement within group performance, which of the following techniques is most related to helping students grow musically?**

a. Assign each student to self-assess their musical strengths and weaknesses.
b. Use a checklist to ensure appropriate posture and instrument holding.
c. Grade students on attendance and perceived participation.
d. Use peers to assess each student's musical achievement.

**57. Which of the following philosophical approaches to music education is David Elliott most associated with?**

a. Praxial music education
b. Utilitarian music education
c. Aesthetic music education
d. Affective music education

**58. Which of the following statements about the music achievement potential of an individual with a disability is most appropriate to consider in teaching and learning music?**

a. Cognitively impaired students generally prefer dancing/singing to playing an instrument.
b. It is generally harder for a student with cognitive impairment to learn how to sing in tune.
c. IQ is a weak predictor of music aptitude and the potential to achieve in music.
d. A student with low music achievement will also have low music aptitude.

**59. Which harmonic texture is best represented by the following music excerpt?**

(J.S. Bach, Fugue in D Minor, BMV Anh 98)

a. Monophonic
b. Homophonic
c. Heterophonic
d. Polyphonic

**60. When reading notation and playing the bass clarinet, in which of the following intervals does the bass clarinet sound lower than the notation?**

a. 12th
b. 10th
c. 9th
d. 8th

**61. When working with ensembles to achieve an appropriate ensemble sound, which of the following sequences of conceptual sonic factors is most appropriate to teach?**

a. Balance, blend, intonation, characteristic sound
b. Blend, balance, intonation, characteristic sound
c. Blend, balance, characteristic sound, intonation
d. Characteristic sound, intonation, blend, balance

**62. Which of the following vocal ranges represents Gordon's initial audiation range for young children?**

a. D5 to A5
b. C4 to G5
c. D4 to A4
d. A4 to F5

**63. Which of the following music terms is best defined as an ornament or embellishment in which the performed note is first brushed—as in a flam—by the note just above it before playing that note for almost its entire value?**

a. Acciaccatura
b. Appoggiatura
c. Upper mordent
d. Tremolo

**64. Which of the following elements is NOT audiated by students?**

a. Intervals
b. Melodic contour
c. Time signatures
d. Harmonic functions

**65. Which of the following reasons for using a backwards design approach to teaching best ensures that instruction meets federal, state, and professional guidelines?**

a. Determining levels of minimal student performance precedes writing goals
b. Developing student learning experiences is derived from standards
c. Writing lesson plans comes before creating assessments
d. Deriving assessments happens after student activities

**66. Which music era is the following music excerpt likely from?**

a. Baroque
b. Classical
c. Romantic
d. Neoclassical

**67. Which of the following musical terms most closely means that the strings are to be struck with the wood of the bow?**

a. Détaché
b. Fuoco
c. Da capo
d. Col legno

**68. Which of the following two tonalities is this melody best characterized by?**

a. Major and Dorian
b. Mixolydian and Aeolian
c. Major and harmonic minor
d. Lydian and melodic minor

**69. Which of the following types of rubrics is most appropriate for measuring a student's understanding, through performance, of the five different types of voices (e.g., singing, speaking, whispering, etc.)?**

a. Additive rating scale
b. Continuous rating scale
c. Numerical rating scale
d. Holistic rating scale

**70. Which of the following rhythm teaching sequences best represents a lower-level elementary school Kodály curriculum?**

a. Fast/slow, *ta/ti-ti*
b. Half-note rest, quarter-note rest
c. Steady beat, fast/slow
d. Upbeat pattern, syncopation

**71. Which pop star used the entirety of Chopin's Prelude Op. 28 No. 20 in C Minor, illustrated below, as the introduction to one of his most popular songs of the 1970s?**

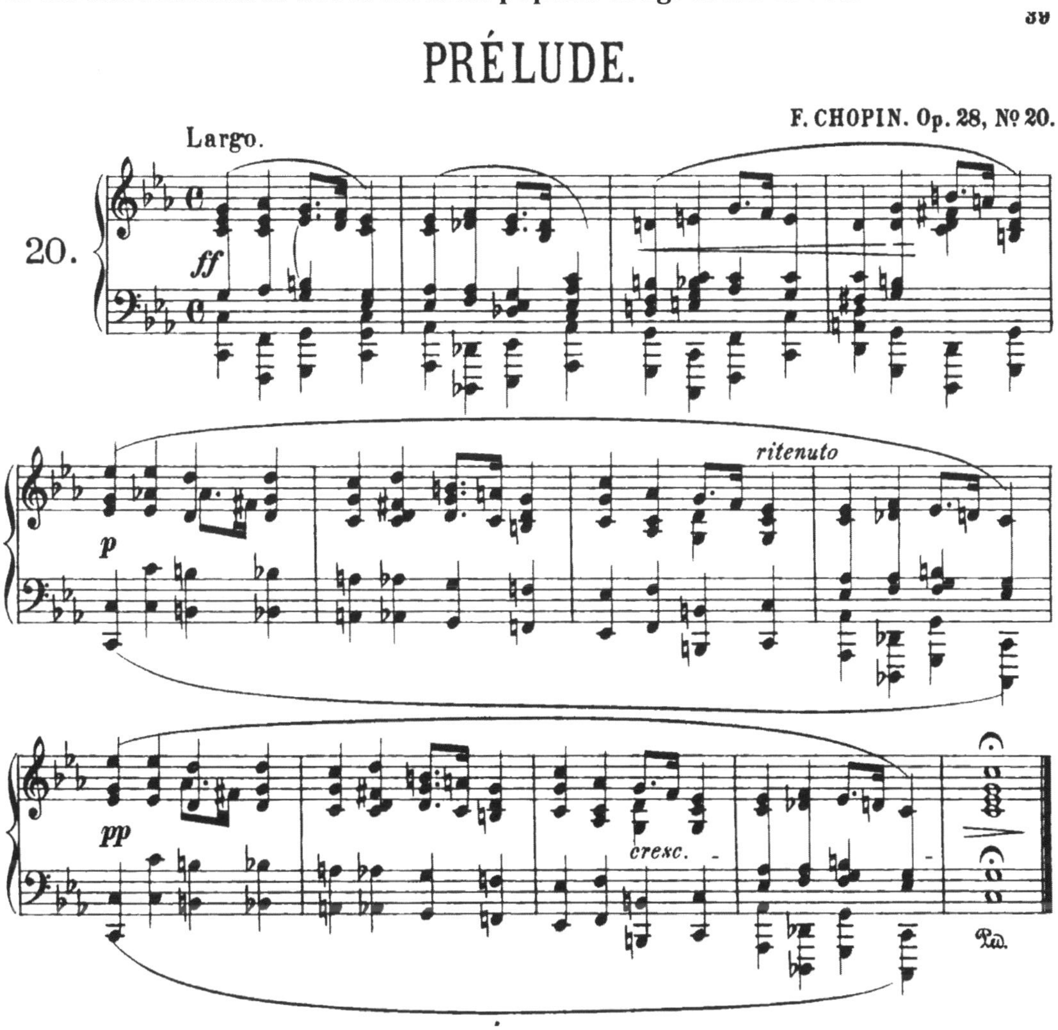


a. Elton John
b. Billy Joel
c. Barry Manilow
d. Neil Diamond

**72. Which of the following range(s) do most double horn players use the Bb side of the instrument for?**

a. Middle register, from C4 to C5
b. Upper register, from C#5 to C6
c. Lower and middle registers, from C3 to C5
d. Lower, middle, and upper registers, from C3 to F3 and G#4 to C6.

**73. In which of the following geographical areas does the art form that employs syllables such as "*ta-ka-di-mi*" originate?**

a. United States
b. Western China
c. Southern India
d. Indonesia

**74. When practicing with drones, which of the following techniques can be used to indicate whether one is playing in-tune with just intonation?**

a. Listening for echo in the room
b. Listening for a core in the center of the tone
c. Listening for others to match pitch
d. Listening for the difference tone

**75. Which of the following fundamental embouchure characteristics applies to all brass instruments?**

a. The tongue says "eeh," and the corners of the lips are pulled back.
b. The tongue is pointed, and the center of the lips is pursed.
c. The corners of the lips are tight and pulled back with a flat chin.
d. The cheeks are puffed, and the chin is rounded.

**76. Which of the following correctly identifies the music excerpt below, for coloratura soprano, and in which opera was it featured?**

a. "O mio babbino caro" from Puccini's *Gianni Schicchi*
b. "Quando me'n vo'" from Puccini's *La bohème*
c. "Non più andrai" from Mozart's *Le nozze di Figaro*
d. "Der Hölle Rache" from Mozart's *Die Zauberflöte*

**77. Which of the following music notation labels are represented in the illustration?**

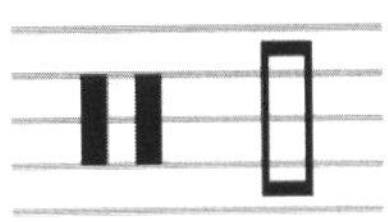

a. Two types of tablature clefs
b. Two types of octave clefs
c. Two types of neutral clefs
d. Two types of treble clefs

**78. Which of the following vocal exercises helps a singer begin to learn how to perform a smooth transition through a vocal break?**

a. Pushing air to support vocal folds
b. Humming warm-ups
c. Closing the mouth to help slow down air flow
d. Enunciation drills

**79. Which of the following differences in special education services is the primary difference between an individualized education plan (IEP) and a 504 plan?**

a. The 504 plan falls under the Individuals with Disabilities Education Act (IDEA) and the IEP does not.
b. The 504 plan is meant to "level the playing field" through accommodations, but an IEP is generally more in-depth.
c. The 504 plan covers students who qualify for special education, and the IEP is to protect against discrimination.
d. The 504 plan must be re-evaluated at least every three years, while law requires only "periodic" re-evaluation of an IEP.

**80. Which of the following pop musicians uses Beethoven's harmonic and melodic structure from the *Pathétique Sonata* in a well-known hit arranged in a doo-wop style?**

a. Elvis Costello
b. Billy Joel
c. Elton John
d. Buddy Holly

**81. Which of the clefs, tonalities, and keys is the following illustrated melody written in?**

a. Bass clef – major – Eb
b. Treble clef – minor – Eb
c. Alto clef – major – Ab
d. Tenor clef – minor – C

**82. Which of the following instructional strategies is the most practical technique to modify music instruction when teaching classical guitar in a general music classroom?**

a. Separate high achievers from low achievers
b. Eliminate individual formative assessments
c. Provide each student with short personal lessons
d. Design group projects based upon mutual interests

**83. Which of the following parent engagement activities is most effective in procuring support from stakeholders?**

a. Building a strong parent booster support group to assist in communicating with other parents, fundraising efforts, chaperoning, and encouraging attendance at performing events
b. Providing weekly emails to parents and community stakeholders with information about upcoming events, awards, dues, and other pertinent program information
c. Creating biannual program dinner/awards ceremonies to establish the importance of the program and celebrate student success
d. Recruiting and establishing an adult performance ensemble in order to engage parental and community support

**84. When teaching and comparing style and form in an ensemble setting, which of the following explanations is most correct?**

a. Forms are subsumed under various styles.
b. Both style and form are largely synonymous.
c. There is a diversity of styles within a particular form.
d. Style represents a time period and form represents musical structure.

**85. In which tonality is the following melody composed?**

a. Phrygian
b. Dorian
c. Lydian
d. Aeolian

**86. Which of the following Western music eras is this music excerpt from, and which genre does it represent?**

a. Medieval; mass
b. Renaissance; motet
c. Renaissance; chanson
d. Baroque; cantata

**87. Which of the following harmonic changes is most appropriate to accompany the following traditional children's song?**

a. I – I – V – I – I - I – V – I
b. i – i – V – i – i – IV – i
c. I – I – V – V – I – I – IV – I
d. I – IV – I – V – I – I – V – I

**88. Which of the following expenditures is a long-term budget item?**

a. Repertoire purchases
b. Uniform upgrades
c. Instrument repair
d. Piano tuning

**89. Which of the following instructional planning techniques is most associated with evidence-centered design (ECD)?**

a. Write unit goals
b. Use backwards mapping
c. Plan learning experiences first
d. Align with national and state standards

**90. Which of the following concert preparations for an upcoming school year is the first behavior that a music teacher should engage in?**

a. Choosing dates for concerts
b. Signing out facilities
c. Preparing a checklist
d. Informing stakeholders of plans

**91. Which of the following middle school choral vocal ranges is most appropriate for male cambiata voices?**

a. G3 to D5
b. A3 to A4
c. C4 to C5
d. D4 to F5

**92. When performing the following music excerpt, which of the following is an area a conductor is most likely to have difficulty with?**

(Stravinsky, *The Rite of Spring,* "The Sacrificial Dance")

a. Navigating the frequent changes in meter while maintaining flowing musicality
b. Maintaining the slow, grave tempo without rushing
c. Maintaining interest with simple textures and harmony
d. Adding grace notes to the various instrument parts

**93. Which of the following four uses of the 6/4 chord does the music excerpt best exemplify?**

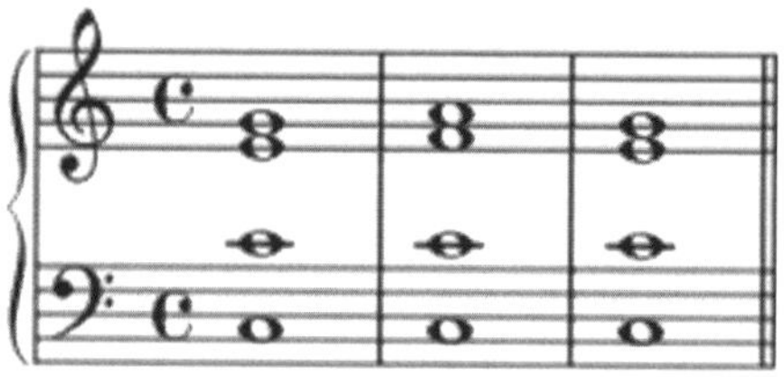

a. Cadential
b. Passing
c. Pedal
d. Arpeggiated

**94. Which of the following conducting patterns best fits the following music excerpt?**

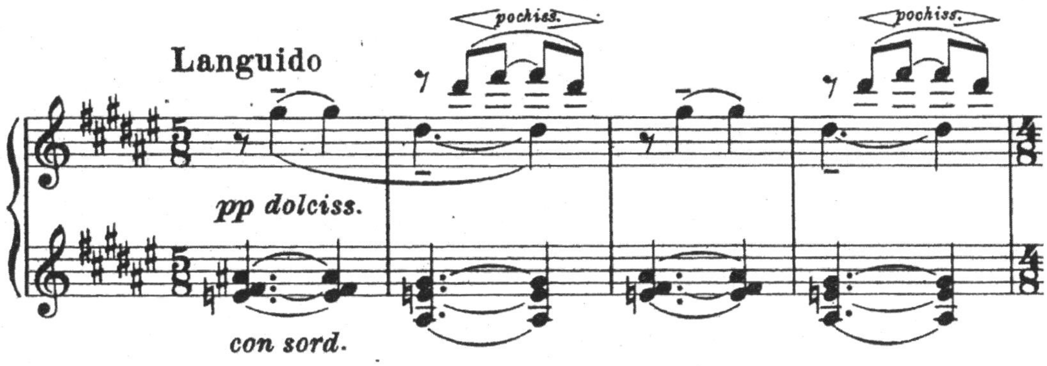


Scriabin Piano Sonata No. 5, Opus 53

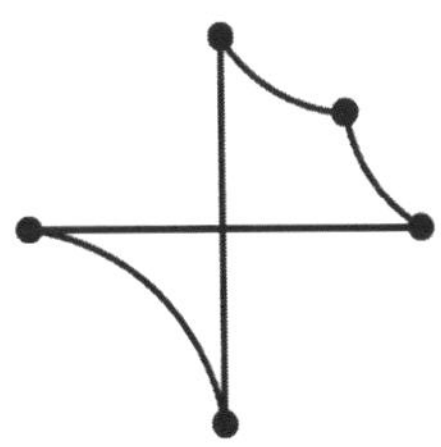

a.

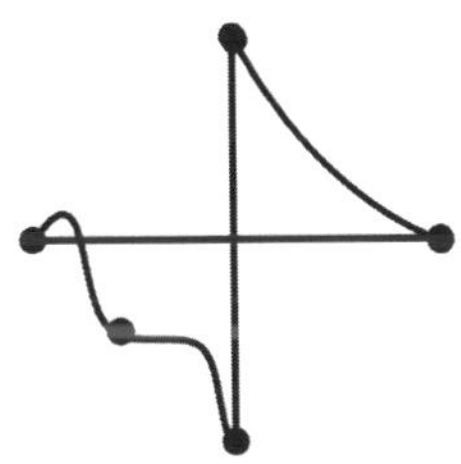

b.

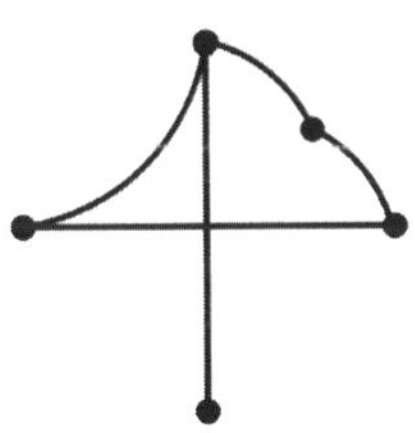

c.

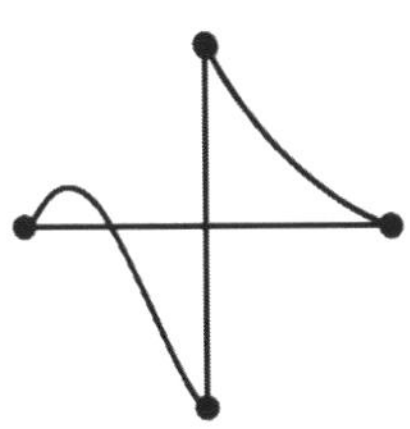

d.

**95. Which of the following tones are affected by pulling out the lower section of a Bb clarinet?**

a. C4 to Bb4
b. E3 to B4
c. G4 to Bb4
d. G3 to G5

**96. Which of the following students are generally most susceptible to hearing loss?**

a. Concert band piccolo players
b. A percussionist in a band class
c. Color guard members attending football games
d. Music appreciation students listening to music during class

**97. Which of the following Western music subgenres is this 20th century music excerpt from?**

a. Neoclassical
b. Impressionism
c. Minimalism
d. Serialism

**98. When teaching small-group instrumental lessons at the middle school level and using Gordon's Learning Sequence Activities, which of the following individualization techniques best teaches to varying student rhythm aptitudes?**

a. Vary the tempos for each student.
b. Vary the meters for each student.
c. Vary the patterns for each student.
d. Vary the tonalities for each student.

**99. Which of the following teaches and guides improvisational skills for both instrumentalists and vocalists, specifically through audiation?**

a. Irv Kratka's "Music Minus One"
b. Christopher Azzara's "Creativity in Improvisation"
c. Jamey Aebersold's "Play-Along"
d. Jerry Coker's "Patterns for Jazz"

**100. Which of the following preparations for a concert is among the last that a music teacher does when preparing for a concert?**

a. Procuring chaperones and other adults to help supervise
b. Send special invitations to administrators
c. Confirm that lights are focused
d. Design the concert program

# Answer Key and Explanations for Test #1

**1. D:** While all of the options may be taught to beginning students to use when practicing, students who are taught to be self-regulated in their learning evaluate their performance; identify what is needed to improve; then plan, monitor, and evaluate strategies they use to do so. Students who demonstrate self-regulated behavior are self-motivated to improve.

Option B is incorrect because breaking the music down into parts may help isolate more difficult passages to be practiced more slowly and more often, but the technique is of little use without self-monitoring. The same principle applies to breaking practice into many short sessions and establishing a routine.

**2. B:** The gamelan ensemble is the traditional ensemble music of Javanese, Sundanese, and Balinese in Indonesia. The gamelan orchestra contains tuned percussion instruments like bells, gongs, drums, and metallophones. It is used for celebratory, religious, and political purposes.

**3. C:** *Piacere* means the performer is able to play as they please. *Niente* means to fade away to nothing. *Battuta* means to return to a normal tempo (*battuto* means to strike the strings on a stringed instrument with the bow). *Cappella* means to perform without instrumental accompaniment.

**4. A:** Because sonata form modulates to different keys (and tonalities), if the ensemble is to perform using beatless just intonation, it is impossible for all instrumentalists to perform to their own instrument's compromised tuning system, which resembles as close as possible the compromise of equal temperament made among the 12 tones that instrument manufacturers make. Also, because sonata form ends in the original key, it is important for ensembles to avoid straying too far from equal temperament in order to end a piece with the same fundamental reference pitches in the original key. Thus, it is important for instrumentalists who play the fundamental tones within a key (e.g., the tonic) to stay as close to equal temperament as possible throughout key and tonality changes, while other players compromise and adjust to the changes throughout. In the end, it must be acknowledged that tuning is a matter of compromise in order to perform beatless harmonies.

**5. A:** Option B, a licensing administrator, oversees copyrights and licenses music, usually working for a publishing company. Option C, an agent, establishes relationships with venue owners and books jobs for musicians. Option D, an artist manager, negotiates business deals on behalf of the artist. An artist manager can work independently or for an artist management company.

**6. B:** Orff seemed to have a general belief that individual human development (ontology) followed the development of the species (phylogeny). That is, at least in part, why he called simple songs "elemental music." This is also why a strong and pronounced rhythmic drive that impels motion and emotion plays a dominant role in his music and thinking about how to engage children in music. One can hear this in his compositions (e.g., *Carmina Burana*). Orff's primary thinking about elemental music is related to the idea that music and movement are elemental modes of expression first and foremost, and that creating an approach to music exploration, performance, and learning based upon this helps children to discover themselves and who they are in relation to people and nature around them. Piaget, among others, was influenced by the 18th century idea of development described in option b), and his stage theory of childhood development reflects this. Option c) is incorrect because Orff did not create a systematic method (what a teacher does, why she does it, and when) so much as an approach for children to discover and create music in order to enrich themselves throughout their lives.

**7. A:** Lifting and arching the tongue speeds up the airflow, like placing a thumb across the opening of a water hose. Reducing the air pressure—the volume of air—causes the aperture to naturally become smaller, like closing the nozzle on a hose. Eventually, the volume of air can be increased after the embouchure has become stronger. This is done by increasing the volume of air by expelling via the stomach muscles. Mouthpiece pressure has a small role to play in this because the aperture becomes smaller as more pressure is exerted on the lips; however, it is physically unhealthy to significantly increase mouthpiece pressure, and it also constricts the sound.

**8. A:** Verdi's opera *Otello* premiered in 1887 and was based on Shakespeare's *Othello*. It was Verdi's second-to-last opera. Gioachino Rossini also wrote a well-known opera called *Otello*, but his version was not based on Shakespeare's *Othello*.

**9. D:** A quaver is equal to an eighth note. Every time a descriptor term is added, it cuts the note value in half (e.g., a semiquaver is equal to a 16th note).

**10. D:** The excerpt above is Ottorino Respighi's *Fountains of Rome* – "The Triton Fountain in the Morning" ("La fontana del Tritone al mattino"). Neoclassicism is characterized by a return to aesthetics of balance and form (hence Respighi's fascination with the four sculpted fountains). Neoclassicism was a reaction against the perceived imbalance of economy and the lack of emotional restraint inherent during the Romantic era; however, compared to the Classical era, the Neoclassical era incorporated expanded instrumentation and harmonic colors.

**11. C:** This lesson process can easily be expanded to include further reflection, creation, and improvisation with various accompaniments, additional sections to the composition, etc. This process allows for music skills to emerge organically during the process as students are developmentally ready to use them. This is an integral component of the Orff approach, as Carl Orff was adamant that Orff Schulwerk be child-centered rather than subjected to the arbitrary and often unimaginative music education practices that are so common. This approach is holistic and embraces the totality of the human experience, enriching children's lives and their future approach to living in the world.

**12. A:** Option B is incorrect because key height is usually checked for leaks in the tone holes and for appropriate venting. For example, if a key is too low, it creates a stuffy sound by blocking the air flow out of the key hole. Adjusting key height is also used to correct intonation problems on one or several keys on the flute; however, it is generally not a first step in tuning a flute, as manufacturer specifications are generally close to the correct height. Flute players often wish to lower the distance between the key and keyhole to increase speed and dexterity.

Option C is incorrect because adjusting the head-joint is done after ensuring that the head-joint cork is in the correct position. Further, concert D5 is often used, particularly for beginning and intermediate students, because the note is not very bendable and both hands are balanced on the flute. Option D is incorrect because changing the angle to raise or lower a pitch is done only as a fine-tuning technique, primarily to account for individual pitch tendencies on a particular flute, as tone problems can become an issue when rolling the flute. The best initial step is to check that the head-joint cork is in the right place with the cleaning rod, as this ensures that the flute's internal tuning is set.

**13. C:** The Picardy third was used as early as the 15th to 17th centuries but also during the Romantic era. Chopin prepares for the Picardy third at the end of the music with falling thirds, setting up a dominant function, followed by the repetition of the Bb major tonic harmonic function at the end.

**14. A:** Modular rotation is achieved by modulating by major or minor thirds, avoiding the more traditional modulations in Western music and helping to create a distinctly Russian sound. Mussorgsky is often considered the most significant composer in characterizing the Russian style of the "Mighty Five."

**15. B:** Option B is correct because quality beginner guitars are significantly more expensive than quality beginner ukuleles. Option A is incorrect because both guitars and ukuleles are made from wood and are subject to cracking in low humidity environments, such as classrooms that are heated throughout the winter months or constantly cooled because of the geographic location. Relatively cheap dehumidifiers may be purchased to keep with these instruments. It should also be noted that keeping these instruments in high humidity can also cause damage. Option C is incorrect because there is no objective evidence or research to validate this statement. Option D is incorrect because guitars have a greater range of tone than ukuleles, which may prompt some music teachers to teach guitar instead of ukulele.

**16. C:** The pickup measure spells an A Major or a I chord. The first beat in the first measure is another spelling of a root position A Major chord. Ignoring the passing eighth note, the notes on the second beat spell a first inversion D Major chord with F# in the bass or $IV^6$. The third beat is a root position E Major chord or V chord. The notes on the fourth beat spell a B minor or a ii minor in root position with B in the bass. In the second measure, the chord on beat one is an A Major chord in first inversion with C# in the bass or a $I^6$. The chord on beat 2 is an E Major chord in root position or a V. Finally, the last chord in our analysis with the fermata is A Major in root position or a I.

**17. A:** Two essential rules for woodwind fingerings are:

1. Don't slide fingers

2. Don't lift fingers on one hand while pressing fingers on the other hand

Choices C and D would require lifting up a finger on the left hand while placing a finger down with the right hand, then doing the opposite after leaving the Bb. Choice B would require sliding with the fingers of the left hand.

**18. D:** While it is important to involve students as stakeholders in as many music council positions as possible, the handling of uniform and instrumental rental fees, concert ticket sales, fundraising revenue, and other monetary issues should be exclusively handled by an adult. If large sums of money are involved, that adult should be bonded—being bonded means that the individual has been purchased a guarantee of payment from a bonding company in the event of mistakes or mishandling of large sums of money.

**19. A:** Even when teaching with traditional, non-audiation-based method books and learning first to decode notes on a staff with letter names, students should learn to pull out their third valve slide. In the same way that many teachers use tape on the fretboard to help string players play in tune even when they cannot audiate, trumpet teachers should be engaging in kinesthetic training as well as establishing good performance habits. If a teacher implements audiation-based methods and techniques into beginning instrumental music lessons, the student will generally not tolerate performing out of tune.

**20. A:** Option A is correct because students can learn to accompany themselves while singing songs. Option B is incorrect because both the recorder and the ukulele can sound pleasant in group settings. (In particular, see Richard Grunow and Edwin Gordon's *Jump Right in: The Instrumental Series* for recorder. It teaches the recorder while also teaching audiation, which improves recorder performance.) Option C is incorrect because this is a subjective rationale: there has been little or no published objective experimental research that justifies this statement. Option D is incorrect because both the ukulele and the soprano recorder can be used in an Orff Instrumentarium. The recorder has a long history in Western European music, beginning in the Middle Ages, and continues to be popular throughout the country and in American culture.

**21. C:** Procuring information about an established program helps to ensure a smooth transition. Topics to be discussed include fundraising, student make-up, student leadership positions, previous concert programs and repertoire, organization handbook, and the booster organization, among other topics.

**22. C:** There are three general types of portfolios, each with distinct purposes, but they also overlap in some areas. These are the working portfolio, the display portfolio, and the assessment portfolio. Option C is the correct answer because the primary purpose of a working portfolio is to be a repository of work that can be used by both the student and the teacher to reflect on a student's strengths and weaknesses and to help the student reflect upon their own achievement, feelings, and beliefs regarding the content contained within. Option A is incorrect because that is a description of a display portfolio, also known as a showcase portfolio. Option B is incorrect because that is a description of an assessment portfolio. Option D is incorrect because that is a description of a hybrid working/assessment portfolio.

**23. A:** Singing root harmonies helps students to lock in singing in-tune, and provides the context of harmonic function for students to use while learning to audiate and sing harmony.

**24. D:** Following the bass line is a good first step to analyzing and deciding which option is the correct answer. Passing tones and other ornamental notes are not integral to the harmonic progression and are not included in the analysis.

**25. C:** Option C is correct because root position part-writing provides a readiness to learn about modulations. Options A, B, and D are incorrect because they are backwards in sequence. Each concept is designed to provide readiness for the next concept and/or taught along with the evolution of practices over time, and is designed to promote a deeper understanding of common practice period standards.

**26. A:** Memorizing common practice period rules is recall of information. Option B is incorrect because comprehension is about understanding the meaning, translation, interpolation, and interpretation of instructions and problems. A student that can state a problem in their own words shows comprehension. Option C is incorrect because application is when a student uses a taught concept in a new situation, an unprompted use of an abstraction, in the classroom, or from readings during novel situations. Option D is incorrect because analysis is what happens when a student separates material or concepts into component parts so that the organizational structures may be understood (an extension of application). A student that distinguishes between facts and inferences shows analysis.

**27. D:** While a combination of all of the options in relationship to the individual player contributes to the type of sound being made, the configuration of the mouthpiece tip, lay, rails, and particularly the baffle contribute more to the sound than the other options, and at a more practical and cheaper price, especially when asking all students to play on the same brand and model instrument, which is not very practical.

A baffle can be a "flat" baffle (producing a darker, thicker, warmer sound with less projection); a "roll-over" baffle (producing a middle-of-the-road sound); or a "step" baffle (producing brighter, louder, and a more projected sound). A flat baffle allows more air to pass through the mouthpiece at once, but at a slower speed. A step baffle is curved, which speeds up the airflow but allows less air to travel through the mouthpiece at once.

**28. B:** Beginning clarinet players have not yet mastered the embouchure development or technical skills required to play the lowest notes of the clarinet or to play over the break. G4 allows the performer to establish the basis for the clarinet performing in tune with itself (because the note is an open note between the barrel and the first joint), as well as secure a reference pitch from the ensemble. G4's pitch tendency is sharp. G3 uses the left-hand assembly and allows the player to continue to place the instrument in tune with itself because it does not affect the left-hand portion of the clarinet. Options (A), (C), and (D) are incorrect because either the notes are too low, go over the break, begin with the right hand, or some combination of these.

**29. B:** The caesura is an untimed break between verses or phrases. Many musicians call this symbol "railroad tracks." The pause may be ever so slight or lengthened for different effect.

**30. B:** The oboe uses the treble clef. The tenor trombone uses the bass and tenor clefs. The Eb baritone saxophone uses the treble clef but sounds an octave and a major sixth lower than what is read. Parts for the viola are typically written in the alto clef, so violists must be able to read this clef.

**31. B:** Synthetic reeds keep a consistent sound over time, whereas cane reeds deteriorate in sound quality after being worn in to their "sweet spot." Option A is incorrect because they do not need to be wet in order to be played. Option C is incorrect because they keep their shape much longer than cane reeds. Option D is incorrect because how they sound is subjective—the quality of synthetic reeds used to be considered by most to be inferior, but that has changed with new technologies. Many persons now prefer the sound of a synthetic reed, or cannot tell the difference (synthetic reeds usually sound a little brighter than cane reeds).

**32. B:** The standard English horn sounds a fifth lower than notated, so it is considered a transposing instrument in F. Other double reed instruments include the oboe and bassoon, both pitched in C and sound as written.

**33. D:** The pattern in answer choice D allows for a meaningful introduction and a fast-paced rehearsal that builds to a final climax, creating a gestalt and synergy in group performance at the end of the rehearsal. A "gestalt" may be defined as the whole being greater, or different, than the sum of the parts. A "synergy" is a gestalt that happens when two or more persons work together to create an idea, product, or process.

Option A is incorrect because students need time to become situated to their surroundings and to warm up their voices and instruments. Option B is incorrect because the curve in the middle goes all the way down, de-energizing the class environment (if it didn't go all the way down, it might be a good model to follow, depending on the class circumstances). Option C is just a variant of Option B.

Any class, whether it is physical education, biology, or music, is best when it builds in intensity towards its intended purpose and climax, then allows students time to synthesize and generalize what they have learned. This is often preceded by a summary section toward the end of a lesson.

The short curve up in the beginning of a lesson is the stakeholder exercise, which often provides a hook for students to cognitively and emotionally hook to.

**34. B:** Homophonic music can have accompaniment that is in the style of block chords, or the accompaniment may have some subjective polyphonic characteristics, such as a guitar accompaniment in pop music in which the performer picks instead of strums. It can also have an accompaniment in which there are harmonic layers. Option A is incorrect because heterophony involves variations of a melodic line played simultaneously. Option C is incorrect because polyphony involves multiple independent melodic lines. Option D is incorrect because it refers to word meaning—lexical semantics—in language. Homonymy refers to words that have the same sound (homophones) or orthographic form

**35. D:** Mixers allow for more control of the input into a computer. Mixers commonly have volume faders, equalizers, and built-in effects such as reverb and delay, and many have an analog-to-digital converter built in. Mixers are therefore better for recording studio use, but because they are less portable, generally more expensive, and more complicated to use than audio interfaces, they may not be the best choice for use in remote recording.

**36. B:** Teaching students to audiate with tonal syllables (moveable *do*, *la*-based minor) and to use those tonal syllables (if needed) when singing a part or when transposing on their instrument allows them to perform tunes and songs learned by rote, by ear, and by notation in any key. Additionally, when students become more advanced in high school, they may use melodies, such as the primary melody in Bach's "Jesu, Joy of Man's Desiring" as a flow and expressive exercise.

**37. D:** Option D is the correct answer because students are being measured on one dimension; however, while it is objectively unknown whether the tonic or the fifth is easier to distinguish and sing (e.g., many students with low music aptitude often sing the fifth), it is clear that distinguishing and singing the third is more difficult. An additive scale has multiple questions that are independently graded, whereas a cumulative scale has interrelated items. Since this checklist has independent scoreable items, it is an additive scale.

**38. C:** Option C is correct because the continuous motion of this excerpt demonstrates the stylistic characteristic of being composed during the Baroque era. Options A and B are incorrect; while basso continuo and polyphonic textures are defining characteristics of the Baroque era, they are not illustrated in this excerpt. Option D is incorrect because this characteristic is more related to music composed in the Classical era.

**39. D:** Modest Mussorgsky's *Pictures at an Exhibition* (1874, a suite of ten pieces plus a variation on the Promenade) was arranged for orchestra by Maurice Ravel in 1922. It was also orchestrated by other composers, such as Sir Henry J. Wood (1915), Leopold Stokowski (1939), and Vladimir Ashkenazy (1982).

**40. C:** This music was probably written for Christmas, 1198 A.D. Pérotin (approximately 1160–1230 A.D.) developed the cantus firmus, which was originally taken from plainchant, to sustain very long notes while the other three voices moved, using the rhythmic modes, above them. Option A is incorrect because it is believed that Pérotin's predecessor, Léonin (1150s A.D. to approximately 1201 A.D.), who was also a composer in the Notre Dame style, was among the first to use the six rhythmic modes that moved in threes. Option B is incorrect because this organum is in four voices. While the cantus firmus ("fixed song") started during the 11th century as plainchant that had a melismatic melody sung over it, Pérotin composed a cantus firmus as the tenor singing a sustained note. Option D is incorrect because this music was composed in the *ars antiqua* style.

**41. B:** Both woodwind and brass instruments, particularly those with a bore, are subject to warm breath being blown into the instrument, causing the instrument to expand and become larger. When an instrument expands, the inside of its bore becomes smaller because the instrument expands inward as well as outward.

Regarding stringed orchestral instruments, humidity levels affect the instrument more significantly than temperature—although there is generally a positive correlation between humidity and temperature. When relative humidity is low, bow hairs shrink and tighten, wooden frames shrink and cause stress on the instrument's parts, soundposts become tighter, and pegs become loose. In relatively higher humidity, the opposite effects occur. On these stringed instruments, temperature affects primarily the strings, which expand—including elongating—requiring tuning adjustments.

**42. C:** In twelve-tone music, the prime row is a series that includes all twelve chromatic pitch classes. Option A is incorrect because notes generally cannot be repeated before the other notes have been played, except for repetition of a note, trills, and tremolos. Option B is incorrect because the order of pitch classes is fixed. Option D is incorrect because there is no fixed order of permutations.

**43. C:** In digital workstations, the maximum dBFS is 0. Anything above 0 dBFS will clip and cause issues such as distortion or loss of signal; therefore, it is best to leave some room for adjustment of levels and aim for around −6 dBFS. While lower peak levels are still usable, aiming for around −6 dBFS is a common practice.

**44. A:** "Desafinado," composed by Antonio Carlos Jobim, with lyrics created by Newton Mendonça, is a song in the bossa nova style, and the title means "out of tune" or "off key." The bossa nova style originated in Brazil in the early 1950s and is a subgenre of samba (a Latin dance subgenre), much like bebop is a subgenre of jazz music.

It's helpful to understand the bossa nova style in relation to its origins in samba. The samba is a subgenre of Latin music that is as much social as it is about musical factors. Samba lyrics speak about collective life, particular notable events, persons, and culture. Samba first appeared in Bahia, Brazil, and was known as the music of slaves.

Musically, the samba is usually played with guitar, bass, and drums. It can include other instruments, including orchestral instruments. The samba is livelier than the bossa nova, but is harmonically simpler, with fewer chord extensions and less complex voicings. Bossa nova uses major and minor seventh and 13th chords and is usually softer and smoother in style and sound. It's generally not danced to as the samba is because it has no formal dance steps. Bossa nova is usually slower in tempo than the samba.

Bossa nova is highbrow samba. Its lyrics are more about the individual and the topic is often about love, loneliness, or living a pleasurable life. The singing voice is less formal and opera-like than samba.

**45. D:** The series is a standard collection for teachers and schools of music. It includes books for beginning band, jazz band, grades 2 through 6 compositions, as well as other factors integral to developing musicianship through a band program. Option A is incorrect as that is a standard text by Shelley Jagow and published by Meredith Music Productions. Option B is incorrect because that is a seminal book for band directors by Edward Lisk. Option C is incorrect because that is a seminal work for performance by James Thurmond.

**46. D:** A retrograde is simply the prime written backwards. In twelve-tone theory, for each twelve-tone row, there is a prime, retrograde, inversion, and retrograde inversion.

**47. B:** Choice B is a vocal practice that produces tension in the tongue. Tension in the tongue produces an affected tone, creates discomfort, reduces range, produces fatigue, and discourages the singer. Choices A, C, and D are all techniques to use when working to alleviate tension in the tongue.

**48. D:** Starting with an "N" consonant before the vowel keeps the voice forward in the mouth and helps to separate the notes, as agility involves smoothness and legato without slurring in between notes. Once a legato style is achieved with adequate abdominal support that does not produce tension at a slower tempo and then a faster tempo, the consonants can be removed. Option B is incorrect because there should be economy of tongue and jaw movement when performing passages that require agile vocalization. Option C is incorrect because learning vocal agility starts with exercises that are relatively slower in tempo.

**49. B:** This excerpt is from the first movement of Franz Joseph Haydn's *Symphony No. 24*. This music is balanced, relatively diatonic, not overly ornamental, lacking in overt emotional expression, and without much polyphony. The instrumentation, stylization, and harmonic content are not indicative of the Romantic or Neoclassical eras.

**50. A:** Kodály advocated beginning with intervals within the pentatonic scale, as his observational research of children was that, during play, children most often chanted *so-mi*, or *so-mi-la*. This is different from singing—think "Ring Around the Rosie," or "na-na-na-na-na-na," which are chants, not songs. Also, Hungarian folk music often incorporated pentatony (with Hungarian-placed intervals). Kodály also believed that half-steps were difficult for children to sing.

**51. A:**

The double ratamacue is: 

The double paradiddle is: 

The flamacue is: 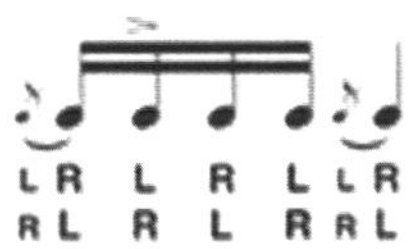


**52. A:** All tuba students should have competencies related to comprehensive musicianship. A challenge for tuba players at all levels of development is the limited nature of their ensemble parts. Tuba parts in ensemble pieces tend to be harmonies or bass lines. This can lead to a lack of practice playing melodic lines. Incorporating more melodic practice can make tuba players more comprehensive musicians. Edwin Gordon and Richard Grunow's *Jump Right In: The Instrumental Series* and Christopher Azzara's *Creativity in Improvisation* series accommodates tuba and other low brass players, affording students the opportunity to become comprehensive musicians.

**53. A:** The US Department Office for Civil Rights, within the "Restraint and Resource Document" published by the US Department of Education, describes two types of restraint: physical and mechanical. Option B is incorrect because "physical escort means a temporary touching or holding of the hand, wrist, arm, shoulder, or back for the purpose of inducing a student who is acting out to walk to a safe location" (p.10). Options C describes a form of mechanical restraint, which is a device used to restrict a student's freedom of movement. Option D describes vehicle safety restraints, which are not considered mechanical restraints when used as intended for transport.

**54. B:** There are three general types of portfolios, each with distinct purposes, but also overlapping in some areas. These are the working portfolio, the display portfolio, and the assessment portfolio. Option B is correct because it is appropriate for an assessment-type portfolio and is grade appropriate. Option A is incorrect because, while it is part of a digital portfolio and is more suitable to a display-type portfolio. Options C and D are incorrect because, while they are both part of a digital portfolio, they are not age appropriate.

**55. A:** When students choose musical instruments based upon the results of a validated timbre preference test, they are more likely to enjoy the timbre of the instrument that they choose, practice more, and stay in instrumental music programs. Option B is incorrect because there may be little relationship between the population of a recruited student's timbre preference(s) and the current instrumentation needs of a particular performing ensemble. Option C is incorrect because, while this is a true reason for using a timbre preference test, it is not as directly related to the primary reason for the use of such a test. Option D is incorrect because the timbre preference test helps gauge which timbres they prefer, and this is not related to the difficulty of the instruments.

**56. A:** Students are most interested in improving their own musicianship and, when given the opportunity, will use rating scales, rubrics, and checklists that are based upon technical and musical factors to self-evaluate their own achievement. Further, there are technical and musical factors listed on standardized adjudication sheets for band, orchestra, choir, show choir, and others that students can use to improve their personal musicianship as well as their musicianship within an ensemble. All students should have copies of these adjudication sheets, as they have the right to know what they will be measured on and how they will be evaluated. The music teacher's responsibility is to help students explore and learn about tuning, intonation, balance, blend, bowing, pronunciation, and enunciation (all the factors on these adjudication sheets) in order to empower students to assess their own strengths and weaknesses. Thus, a music teacher must be musical; a technician on all instruments (including the voice); and be able to communicate, model, diagnose, and prescribe based on the factors on the adjudication sheets, both in individual and group settings. Measuring, evaluating, and grading students based upon attendance and perceived participation is relatively easy in a group setting but does little to promote musical growth. While ensuring appropriate posture and instrument holding is important, allowing students to self-assess their strengths and weaknesses more directly affects musical growth. Using peers who often are lacking in knowledge and skills to assess others could lead to resentment or a lack of group cohesion.

**57. A:** Elliott's philosophy includes the idea that musical works have various meanings for individuals that uniquely contribute to each person's life values.

**58. C:** The correlation between general IQ and various musical aptitudes is between 0.10 and 0.20. In other words, one cannot be predicted from the other. Option A is incorrect because it is a popular stereotype that is often perpetuated by teachers who find it difficult to accommodate teaching musical instruments to students with cognitive impairment. Option B is incorrect because there is a low correlation between the potential to achieve in music (audiationally) and general IQ. Option D is incorrect because, for example, there may be a lot of students at the elementary age level who have not yet learned to sing in tune, or may have had limited exposure to music, but may have high potential to achieve in music. That is, in part, why music teachers use music aptitude tests: to help them see what they may not be hearing.

**59. D:** Polyphonic texture is characterized by multiple melodic lines, all of equal importance, playing simultaneously. Bach's contrapuntal compositions made direct use of polyphonic textures.

A modern example of polyphonic texture is jazz music with interweaving horn lines. The subjective factor is the consideration about how important the accompanying lines are relative to the melody.

**60. C:** The bass clarinet sounds an octave plus the interval of a major second below what is written in the treble clef—a major ninth. This makes it easier for Bb soprano clarinet players to play the bass clarinet, as the fingerings are essentially the same (although the bass clarinet may have a couple of extra notes at the bottom of its range). Because both the soprano clarinet and the bass clarinet are Bb instruments, the bass clarinet sounds one octave lower than a Bb soprano clarinet. Also, because both the bass clarinet and the Bb soprano clarinet are Bb instruments, they sound a major second lower than how they are written for in the treble clef. That is, a written C in the treble clef will sound as a concert Bb. That is why the instruments are Bb instruments.

**61. D:** While individual players' characteristic sounds are unique due to factors ranging from oral cavity to the mouthpiece and instrument being played, there is a general consensus by musicians, musical instrument manufacturers, and music teachers about what a particular instrument's characteristic sound should be. This is evinced by the relatively homogenous sound that most quality instruments produce by players with good embouchures, appropriate breath support, and quality articulation. Intonation is the next factor in the sequence because a section or ensemble cannot achieve blend or balance unless players are performing with instruments that are in tune with themselves and when the players are playing in tune with other members of the ensemble. Blend is related to a characteristic sound and the combination of characteristic sounds within, between, and among sections in order to create a homogenous and sonorous (if not unique) group sound that is different than any individual's characteristic sound. The next factor in the sequence, balance, is primarily a matter of each instrumentalist performing at appropriate volume levels in relation to the sound that they contribute to the section and ensemble.

**62. C:** The initial audiation range is the primary range that teachers should use when singing songs to young children, both before and while these children are first being exposed to music. Children may babble and experiment with their voices above and below this range, however, this perfect fifth was advocated by Gordon because children perceive and respond best to songs and tonal patterns within this range, enabling the music teacher to shape a young child's ability to sing in tune and expand their singing range.

**63. A:** Acciaccatura is an ornament or embellishment that was especially common in the Baroque period, though modern solos and ensemble literature still make use of it. The acciaccatura looks like the following:

**64. C:** Students audiate musical meter and tonality—they internally hear and feel patterns of beat, tonal center, scale degrees, intervals in context, melodic contour, and harmonic functions (e.g., tonic vs. dominant). Time signatures, however, are notation symbols that label meter on the page; they are not perceived directly in inner hearing. Thus, time signatures are not audiated, while the other options are.

**65. B:** The continuum in backwards design starts with standards, then goals and big themes or unifying ideas, then writing measurable objectives and related assessments that define minimal competence, then writing lesson plans and creating student activities and experiences.

**66. B:** This excerpt is the first movement of Franz Joseph Haydn's Symphony No. 24. This music is balanced, relatively diatonic, not overly ornamental, lacking in overt emotional expression, and without much polyphony. The instrumentation, stylization, and harmonic content are not indicative of the Romantic or Neoclassical periods.

**67. D:** *Col legno* means to strike the strings with the wood of the bow, which matches the question stem. *Détaché* means to play the notes separately. *Fuoco* means to play in a fiery manner. *Da capo* means "from the head" (beginning).

**68. B:** The resting tone for Mixolydian is "*so*." The resting tone for Aeolian is "*la*." Characteristic harmonic functions for Mixolydian are I (*so-ti-re*) – IV (*do-mi-so*) – bVII (*fa-la-do*). Characteristic harmonic functions for Aeolian are i (*la-do-mi*) – iv (*re-fa-la*) – bVii (*so-ti-re*).

**69. A:** Option A is the correct answer because an additive rating scale is created so that the criteria are related but not dependent upon one another. Using an additive rating scale, the teacher simply adds the number of criteria that a student achieved and compares it to a continuous rating scale in which a student cannot achieve a 2 unless that student first achieves a 1. Although understanding the different types of voices is related, one may not objectively create a continuous rating scale from these criteria. For example, a student may be able to demonstrate a speaking voice but not a whispering voice, but achievement on one is not dependent on achievement on another. In contrast, an example of a continuous performance rating scale (based on a performance of the melody below) may be:

1. Student performs with steady tempo
2. Student accurately performs division patterns
3. Student accurately performs elongation patterns
4. Student performs with a sense of rubato

In the example above, a student cannot achieve a 2 unless that student first achieves a 1. These types of rating scales are specific and thus more reliable and valid, but may not be appropriate for all performance situations. (See Dalcroze for an explanation of rhythmic, arrhythmic, and eurythmic performances, which are the types of performances measured by this rating scale).

A numeric rating scale is simply a line with numbers that start low and go higher. A holistic rating scale often attempts to mix tonal, rhythmic, and expressive elements, thus precluding the opportunity to focus on a student's specific strengths and weaknesses in performance.

**70. A:** The correct answer is A. In the Kodály method, students begin by experiencing broad rhythmic and tempo contrasts such as fast and slow through movement and listening. They are then introduced to basic rhythm syllables like "ta" and "ti-ti," which form the foundation of rhythm reading. Option B is incorrect because rests are introduced later. Option C is incomplete because it does not progress to rhythm syllables, which are a key component of early Kodály instruction. Option D is incorrect because syncopation and upbeat patterns are more advanced.

**71. C:** Barry Manilow used Chopin to begin his song titled "Could it be Magic" on his debut album, *Barry Manilow*. The song is featured on the first track of the second side of the album. The song was covered in 1992 by the band Take That and peaked at number three on the charts. The song was also covered by Donna Summer in 1976.

**72. B:** The Bb side of the horn is smaller, causing the partials to be further apart in the beginning range and making it easier for beginners to hit the correct notes. Most double horn players use it primarily in the upper register. The Bb side of the horn is engaged by pressing the thumb trigger. Although the fingerings for the F side and the Bb side are mostly different, each side is read with the same notation and sounds the same for each notated note. Because the horn has both the F and Bb sides, and because pitch tendencies associated with the slides and valve combinations make intonation somewhat difficult throughout the register, players can make slight adjustments to pitches with their hand in the bell (the further in, the lower the pitch) and with their embouchure.

**73. C:** In Southern India, konnakol is used by vocal percussion artists to improvise rhythmic compositions. Some in the West have infused konnakol into their popular music as part of a more traditional music structure. Konnakol is differentiated from beatboxing in that, in konnakol, the artist is not attempting to re-create the sound of a percussion instrument.

**74. D:** The difference tone (also known as the Tartini tone) sounds *in the ear* below two tones that are being played together with sustain and intensity. Tartini advocated listening for the difference tone when playing double stops on a stringed instrument in order to achieve good, beatless intonation. Option A is incorrect because room echo does not indicate intonation. Option B is incorrect because a core sound in the center of the tone indicates a developed embouchure and performing in synchrony with the pitch tendencies of a particular instrument, but the core tone does not indicate that one is performing beatless harmonies with a drone. Option C is incorrect because drones are used primarily in individual practice sessions in order for an individual to learn to perform with various temperaments; however, a second player can sometimes perform the drone.

**75. C:** The chin is flat, and even concave, much like it might be when applying lipstick or spitting an apple seed that is caught in the teeth. The corners of the lips are firm, pulled back, and may be pointed slightly downward. Once these two factors are accounted for, the embouchure should naturally fall into place. The next steps are learning how to buzz, then where to place the mouthpiece on the lips and the positioning of the tongue (if it does not come naturally to the player). This basic embouchure technique is also applicable to woodwind instruments, although woodwind instrument embouchures add steps in determining the shape of the lips ("oh")— just like a string at the top opening of a bag is pulled from both sides—and adjusting the lips when placing the mouthpiece or reed inside the mouth. The woodwind embouchure adds steps to the basic formation because, unlike the brass embouchure in which the lips are the sound maker, a reed or double reed is needed to make the sound with woodwinds.

**76. D:** All of the arias listed here are among the greatest arias of all time. Mozart's "The Queen of the Night" from the opera *Die Zauberflöte* ("*The Magic Flute*") is illustrated here at perhaps its most well-known spot, starting with a virtuosic melismatic passage and an exploration of the extreme of the soprano range.

**77. C:** A neutral clef is used for non-pitched instruments. When notating percussion, each line represents a specific instrument. If there is only one non-pitched instrument, a single staff line may be used.

**78. C:** Closing the mouth slows down air flow and reduces air compression. Slowly singing downward through a closed mouth helps the singer to concentrate on making the sound pressure more evenly distributed throughout the register, which is the first step in smoothing out a break. Option A is incorrect because too much pushing with the air puts excess air compression on the vocal folds, exacerbating the break. Option B does not improve transitions through a vocal break as directly as option C. Option D trains enunciation, not transitions through a vocal break.

**79. B:** A 504 plan is for students with disabilities that do not require as much in-depth intervention as students with disabilities who require an IEP. Option A is incorrect because the 504 plan falls under the Rehabilitation Act, Section 504. Option C is incorrect because all special education students are protected from discrimination. Option D is incorrect because it is the IEP that is subject to re-evaluation at least every three years and the 504 plan requires only periodic re-evaluation.

**80. B:** Billy Joel, on his album, *An Innocent Man*, uses harmonic and melodic content from Ludwig van Beethoven's *Piano Sonata No. 8* in C minor, Op. 13 in the chorus on his song, "This Night," and credits Beethoven on the album cover.

**81. A:** The resting tone is *do*, and there are three flats in Eb major. The bass clef is also known as the F clef.

**82. D:** Option D is the correct answer because teachers can group by student preferences when offering choices of tunes or songs that students want to learn, learning about the history and use of the guitar in different cultural settings or genres, and then having the different groups of students present their findings and perform to the rest of the class, etc. Option A is incorrect because high and low achievers learn from one another (often more than they do from the teacher), even when differentiating instruction, such as progressing with tonal and rhythm patterns through Gordon's skill learning sequence, or when assigning students different tunes or songs to learn as homework in order to play for the class, etc. Option B is incorrect because formative assessment assists the teacher in deciding how to differentiate instruction based upon achievement and preferences. Option C is incorrect because it is impractical to provide individual lessons to each student. A better option is to pair high achievers with low achievers for peer coaching.

**83. A:** A strong booster club can help make parents into active partners who help with critical tasks like communication, fund-raising, and chaperoning. This can help make events much more successful and help build a thriving culture around the music program. This is far more effective than leaving the whole program to the work of the faculty or staff members alone.

**84. C:** This rationale clarifies style and form to the nearest extent possible, given that terms about genre, subgenre, form, and style are often confused and can be subjective.

Musical form describes the structure of a music composition. The following list represents common music forms:

- Strophic
- Binary
- Ternary
- Rondo
- Arch
- Sonata

There may be different styles within a particular form. For example, sonata form has developed throughout history. Sonata form developed as the first movement within the musical genre of the sonata. Sonata form was developed primarily during the Classical era, but continued to stylistically evolve throughout subsequent musical eras. For example, Beethoven's use of the sonata form is generally more complex in style, including expanding the development section, than Haydn's use of the sonata form.

**85. B:** Dorian is a minor-type tonality and shares the same notes with Aeolian, except that Dorian has a raised sixth. Moveable *do*, *la*-based minor is used by well-informed music teachers to teach audiation. Fixed *do* is more useful for music theorists. Using moveable *do*, *la*-based minor, Dorian tonality's resting tone is *re*. Characteristic harmonic functions are i (*re-fa-la*) – IV (*so-ti-re*) – bVII (*do-mi-so*). Other characteristic patterns are *do-mi-re* and *ti-so-la*.

**86. B:** This motet is titled *Acceptit Jesus calicem*, by Giovanni Palestrina (1525 A.D.-1594 A.D.). This late Renaissance motet is characterized by its:

- Highly polyphonic nature, with each line being of equal importance
- Imitative quality
- Having Latin text
- Being sacred (although some motets, beginning in the high Medieval period, were composed about courtly love). This motet is based upon "our father," beginning with "*pater noster*." This is in contrast to the mass, which had five parts: Kyrie, Gloria, Credo, Sanctus, Agnus Dei
- Still being relatively modal
- Containing a cantus firmus
- Small jumps, and a stepwise move in the opposite direction after a jump
- Notation that is developed beyond the notation of the Medieval period, and all of the parts are on one sheet of paper
- Characteristic complex music that overtakes the text
- Fluid style rather than static in movement
- Dissonances that are confined to suspensions

**87. A:** The song is in major tonality and uses the tonic and dominant harmonic functions.

**88. B:** Options A, C, and D are short-term expenditures. Short-term expenditures are typically defined as costs that are repeating and that take place every year. Long-term expenditures are more expensive items that require a plan to save for over a period of time. Uniform upgrades are long-term expenditures because they are large, infrequent costs.

**89. B:** Backwards design was created to improve learning outcomes by explicitly creating those outcomes first, rather than simply creating activities and then the assessment, which leads to poor achievement of goals and objectives. Evidence-centered design (ECD) is about ensuring that the evidence of achievement is planned before creating learning activities and experiences that lead students to the achievement of those goals and objectives.

**90. C:** Options A, B, and D should be a part of that initial checklist. Other preparations should be procuring music and teaching materials, procuring or designating performance attire and rules for behavior, arranging for chaperones, and making plans for the concerts to be recorded, among other plans.

**91. B:** The cambiata (changing voice) for the choral voice is subject to a more limited range and inconstancy in response. Male cambiata (changing) voices typically have a usable range of about A3 to F4, with a limited tessitura. Among the options given, A3 to A4 (choice B) best reflects this lower, restricted range, whereas the other ranges extend too high for most changing male voices. There are also emotional factors to consider in order to promote a successful and satisfying experience to middle school boys.

**92. A:** This part of Igor Stravinsky's *The Rite of Spring*, first performed in Paris under the baton of Pierre Monteux in 1913, is considered extremely difficult to conduct because of the speed with which the metric changes take place. Conductors may struggle to navigate these changes while maintaining musicality. Option B is incorrect because this section does not have a slow tempo. Option C is incorrect because the textures and harmony of this section are complex. Option D is incorrect because the conductor does not add grace notes.

**93. C:** Each of the 6/4 chords (cadential, passing, pedal and arpeggiated) have different characteristics and serve different purposes, but they are all 6/4 chords that are integrally related to the harmonic functions on each side of the chord. In the pedal 6/4:

- The pedal 6/4 chord has the same harmonic functions as the chords that it embellishes.
- The outer harmonic functions are in root position (e.g., I – $IV^{6/4}$ – I, or V – $i^{6/4}$ – V).
- Upper voices move by step up, then back down.
- The pedal 6/4 chord falls on a metrically weak beat, so although one may accent it in performance, one would not emphasize it in audiation in order to perceive meter.

**94. B:** Scriabin's (1871-1915) fifth piano sonata was composed in 1907, and the above excerpt is the second theme. The music is marked *Languido*, which means sluggish, spiritless. The bass clef provides the best direction for conducting, as it is in a 3+2 pattern, and the music is slow enough so that the treble clef can easily follow this pattern. Option A is a 4+1 pattern. Option C is a 1+4 pattern. Option D is a 2+3 pattern.

**95. B:** E3 to B4 represents the tones fingered on the lower section of a Bb clarinet. The principle is that, as each joint is adjusted from the first joint downward, each of the notes below that joint are affected.

**96. A:** Decibel (dB) levels, length of produced sound, and frequency levels are the primary factors in damage to hearing. All options except for option A can be relatively controlled, but a piccolo player in a concert band situation is typically performing indoors and in the front of the ensemble, and the placement of the instrument is not a factor that can be controlled.

**97. D:** Serialism is a subgenre within classical music, specifically the era of 20th century Classical music. This piece, titled *Die Maschine*, Op. 1, was composed by Fritz Heinrich Klein (1892–1977). It was published in 1921, and the style is indicative of serialistic composers' presentation of the twelve tones, which includes the techniques of retrograde, inversion, and transposition.

Twelve-tone music is performed by orchestras using equal temperament, as each note is considered equal in value, with the distance between notes being a significant factor. All 12 pitches are arranged in a specific sequence.

**98. C:** One of the most significant factors in Gordon's approach to music teaching and learning is that students with low, medium, and high aptitudes should first be taught easy, moderate, and difficult patterns, respectively. When teaching Gordon's Learning Sequence Activities, tonal and rhythm aspects are separated, in part because an individual's tonal aptitude is usually different from her rhythm aptitude. Rhythm patterns are heard, echoed with a neutral syllable, then echoed with rhythm syllables before being read and written. Then, they are read and written in chains of patterns. After that, students learn to identify unfamiliar patterns aurally and in notation based upon the familiar patterns that they have learned by rote. Finally, students create and improvise based upon audiation rather than exploration or through music theory. Music theory is the last part of the learning sequence, just as formalized grammar is acquired after initially learning to listen, speak, read, and write in language learning.

**99. B:** Christopher Azzara's "Creativity in Improvisation" series focuses on audiation-based techniques to help students improve their improvisational skills. "Music Minus One" is similar to karaoke in that a student performs the missing part on a recording. "Play-Along" encourages the memorization, experimentation, and application of scales along with recorded tunes as one teaches him or herself to improvise through aleatory experience. "Patterns for Jazz" is a popular book with patterns that a musician transposes to different keys and uses while learning to improvise through experimentation and self-teaching.

**100. C:** Though these steps are not required to be done in any particular time frame, the most likely of these steps to be performed at the last minute is to focus the lights as it pertains to the final setup of the staging. The other steps allow for too much room for failure if they are performed at the last minute. Procuring supervision and sending invitations to administration are done approximately two weeks before the concert. Designing the concert program is done between one and two weeks before the performance. Focusing the lights and setting up the stage, warmup room and rehearsal rooms are among the last teacher behaviors to do on a well-organized checklist.

# Practice Test #2

**1. Which of the following justifications for the performance of religious music, such as Mozart's *Requiem*, is the most appropriate for a high school choral director to use?**

a. It is classical music.
b. It is standard quality literature.
c. The students want to perform it.
d. The community is predominantly Christian.

**2. For intermediate to advanced clarinet players, which pair of notes provides the most appropriate reference points for tuning a clarinet to itself?**

a. G4, C5
b. E3, C5
c. E3, B4
d. B4, G4

**3. Which of the following concert pitches should sound when playing on the clarinet barrel and mouthpiece alone?**

a. F#
b. Bb
c. Ab
d. E

**4. Which of the following Latin names is the following note called?**

a. Crotchet
b. Minim
c. Semibreve
d. Breve

**5. Which of the following composers wrote the famous melody seen in the lower strings of the following music excerpt?**

a. Mozart
b. Mahler
c. Beethoven
d. Schubert

**6. Given the order of notes within the following music excerpt, which style of music is this most likely to be?**

a. Impressionist
b. Serialist
c. Neoclassical
d. Minimalist

**7. Which of the following multiple-copy rules is allowed under the 1976 Copyright Act?**

a. Copies omit notice of copyright
b. Copies of complete poems less than 275 words
c. Copies fall under the brevity, spontaneity, and cumulative effect rule
d. Copies include no more than two charts, diagrams, or drawings per book

**8. The hymn illustrated below, *Ut queant laxis*, is significant for which of the following reasons?**

**Translation:**

So that your servants may, with loosened voices, resound the wonders of your deeds, clean the guilt from our stained lips, O Saint John.

a. It was used to teach solmization.
b. It was composed for John the Baptist.
c. The melody was composed by Guido d'Arezzo.
d. It was the first example of modern music notation.

**9. Which of the following is the minimum appropriate performance duration for students performing grade level 4 band literature?**

a. 9 minutes
b. 6 minutes
c. 10 minutes
d. 12 minutes

**10. Which of the following "Mighty Five" compositional techniques is used in the following music excerpt?**

(Alexander Borodin, *Prince Igor*)

a. Pentatonic scale
b. Fragmentation
c. Heterophony
d. Diminution

**11. Which of the following philosophers in music education is most associated with aesthetic music education?**

a. Edwin Gordon
b. Susanne Langer
c. Bennett Reimer
d. John Dewey

**12. Mainstreaming and inclusion are concepts included in which of the following parts of the Individuals with Disabilities Education Act (IDEA)?**

a. Least restrictive environment (LRE)
b. Free Appropriate Public Education (FAPE)
c. Individualized education program (IEP)
d. Present levels of performance (PLP)

**13. Which of the following two tonalities is the following notated melody in?**

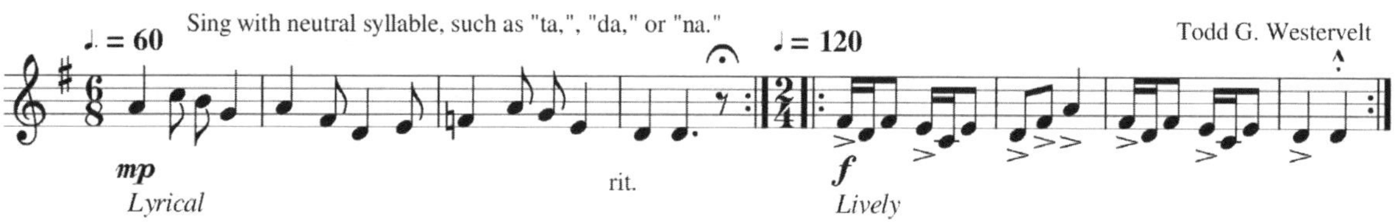


a. Aeolian and major
b. Mixolydian and major
c. Dorian and Mixolydian
d. Dorian and Aeolian

**14. Which of the following types of row forms used in 12-tone music is the upside-down permutation of the original tone row?**

a. Prime
b. Retrograde
c. Inversion
d. Retrograde inversion

**15. A student choral committee is planning a year-end banquet and wants to create a video montage of graduating seniors throughout the year. Which of the following types of copyright license will allow the committee to use copyrighted music performances to play over the video?**

a. Grand license
b. Mechanical license
c. Compulsory license
d. Synchronization license

**16. Which of the following major leaders in music education suggested that *a cappella* singing and native folk songs should be the primary means for children to gain music understanding?**

a. Kodály
b. Gordon
c. Orff
d. Dalcroze

**17. Which of the following reasons for using an F attachment on a Bb trombone relates to improving agility?**

a. Allows sixth position notes to be played in first position
b. Allows fifth position notes to be played in first position
c. Allows fourth position notes to be played in first position
d. Allows third position notes to be played in first position

**18. Which of the following steps for a middle-D not "speaking" correctly on a saxophone should be done first when diagnosing this problem?**

a. Look at the G# key to see if it's stuck.
b. Examine the octave key mechanism.
c. Play just the reed/mouthpiece setup.
d. Run a leak light to check for pad seating.

**19. Compared to a condenser microphone, which of the following reasons is the best for choosing a dynamic microphone?**

a. Greater sensitivity and output
b. No need for phantom power
c. Better suited for the studio
d. Better suited for higher frequencies

**20. When an alto saxophone player begins to double on a Bb soprano clarinet, which of the following embouchure differences should be accounted for?**

a. The lips should be pulled further back for the clarinet.
b. The mouthpiece should be taken in more for the clarinet.
c. The corners of the embouchure should be firmer for the clarinet.
d. The chin should be more pulled down and concave for the clarinet.

**21. Which of the following piano fingering patterns is for right hand C major scale?**

a. 2, 1, 2, 3, 1, 2, 3, 4
b. 1, 2, 3, 1, 2, 3, 4, 5
c. 5, 4, 3, 2, 1, 3, 2, 1
d. 3, 2, 1, 4, 3, 2, 1, 3

**22. Which of the following physical actions meant to seclude a student best legally defines "physical seclusion"?**

a. Involuntary confinement of a student alone in a room in which the student is physically prevented from leaving
b. A timeout, used as a behavior management technique that is part of an approved program
c. Monitored separation of a student in a non-locked setting and implemented for the purpose of calming
d. Confining a student to a locked-down area during an emergency situation, such as the presence of a school shooter

**23. When marking a music composition's form on a rehearsal/preparation score, which of the following rehearsal score preparation sequences is listed in the correct order when planning for ensemble rehearsals?**

a. Determine form; mark motifs and phrases.
b. Mark large sections; mark periods and cadences.
c. Mark periods and cadences; mark motifs and phrases.
d. Mark large sections; determine form.

**24. Which of the following instructional planning sequences is most appropriate in instructional design that accounts for federal, state, and professional guidelines?**

a. Standards, assessments, lesson plans
b. Measurable objectives, student experiences, goals
c. Defining minimal competence, assessments, activities
d. Big themes, standards, lesson plans

**25. Which of the following program evaluation techniques is most useful when done at the state or even national level, rather than the local level?**

a. Well-seasoned subject matter experts (SMEs) make judgments about the worth of a program.
b. Standardized tests of music achievement are administered to students in all music classes.
c. Administrators make professional development recommendations based upon contest results.
d. Music advocacy groups write standards and make recommendations for materials and equipment.

**26. Which of the following expressive markings means the same thing as the following music sign?**

>

a. ***sfz***

b. ***ff***

c. ***mf***

d. ***fp***

**27. Which of the following countries does the cajon come from?**

a. Mexico
b. Mali
c. Peru
d. Jamaica

**28. Which of the following ensemble rehearsal descriptions is most important to maximize learning?**

a. Alternating between breaking the music down and building it back up
b. Making sure that there is a high play-to-talk ratio
c. Including sight-reading every practice session
d. Slowing rehearsal pace to stay focused

**29. The Classical era and the Baroque era have distinct stylistic characteristics. Which of the following characteristics displayed in the following excerpt distinguishes it as a Baroque work?**

(Bach's Brandenburg Concerto No. 1 in D Major, BWV 1046)

a. Figured bass
b. Changing mood
c. Balanced phrasing
d. Terraced dynamics

**30. Which of the following beginning sequences to tune a double horn is most appropriately used after completely pushing in all the slides?**

a. Tune the Bb side of the horn with a tuner using a note that shares the same fingering on both sides of the horn with C5 (concert F4). Then tune the F side to the Bb side using the same note.
b. Tune the F side of the horn with a tuner using a note that it shares the same fingering on both sides with C5 (concert F4). Then tune the Bb side to the F side using the same note.
c. Tune the Bb side of the horn with a tuner using F5 (concert Bb3). Then tune the F side to a tuner using C4 (concert F4).
d. Tune both the Bb and the F sides of the horn with a tuner to E6 (concert A). Then proceed through prescribed valve combinations, starting with the first valve B4 (concert E).

**31. When overblowing a musical instrument, which of the following overblows at the 12th rather than at the octave?**

a. Saxophone
b. Clarinet
c. Trumpet
d. Flute

**32. Which of the following musical textures is best represented by the music excerpt below?**

a. Monophonic
b. Homophonic
c. Heterophonic
d. Polyphonic

**33. Which of the following harmonies is most appropriate to accompany measures 1 and 2 of the following traditional children's music song?**

a. I – iii – IV – V
b. I – IV – I – IV
c. I – iii – V – IV
d. I – I – IV – I

**34. Which of the following subtests from the Iowa Tests of Music Literacy (ITML) achievement battery requires students to indicate the chord progressions that they are listening to?**

a. Tonal audiation/listening
b. Tonal audiation/reading
c. Tonal audiation/writing
d. Tonal audiation/improvising

**35. What 1953 Broadway musical featured the following melody from Alexander Borodin's opera *Prince Igor* and was later covered by such pop stars as Tony Bennett, Johnny Mathis, and Nat King Cole?**

a. *Carousel*
b. *Anything Goes*
c. *Damn Yankees*
d. *Kismet*

**36. Who of the following is credited with composing the following Requiem excerpt?**

a. Wolfgang Mozart
b. Luigi Cherubini
c. Michael Haydn
d. Hector Berlioz

**37. Why might a progressive music teacher who emphasizes solfege advocate for a beginning baritone student to learn to read both treble and bass clef simultaneously?**

a. If a student is proficient in interpreting solfege, transposing between the two clefs becomes fairly easy.
b. Beginning music for the baritone is written in treble clef.
c. Baritone players often switch from playing trumpet.
d. Using treble clef eliminates the use of ledger lines.

**38. Which of the following clefs, tonalities, and keys is the following melody written in?**

a. Tenor clef – Dorian – E
b. Tenor clef – minor – E
c. Alto clef – major – D
d. Alto clef – Mixolydian – G

**39. Which of the following concert keys is a standard baritone saxophone pitched in?**

a. Concert Bb
b. Concert Eb
c. Concert F
d. Concert G

**40. Students pretend to pick up and drink a teacup filled with tea. Then, students pretend to pick up a teacup filled with liquid lead. Which of Laban's effort elements are most directly changed?**

a. Weight and flow
b. Time and space
c. Weight and space
d. Time and flow

**41. Which of the following tongue tension-releasing exercises best forms the basis for all exercises that help to release tension in the tongue?**

a. Drinking lukewarm water to relax the tongue before vocalizing
b. Stretching the tongue using various techniques
c. Releasing tongue and jaw tension with massages and breathing exercises
d. Rolling the neck and head, keeping the mouth open and jaw down when rolling the head back

**42. Which of the following software applications is commonly thought of as the industry standard for professional music notation?**

a. MuseScore
b. GarageBand
c. Dorico
d. Cubase

**43. Which of the following budget methods helps ensure long-term continued supply of working equipment and instruments?**

a. Regular repair and maintenance
b. Educating students about appropriate care of materials
c. Fundraising activities and dues collection on a regular basis
d. Depreciating and amortizing capital supplies while planning for replacement

**44. When a music teacher works with young, beginning instrumentalists by having them focus on hearing and internalizing music (audiation) through listening activities and playing music by ear before being introduced to music notation, they are following the learning theory of which music educator?**

a. Suzuki
b. Gordon
c. Dalcroze
d. Kodály

**45. Which of the following jazz standards is performed in the bossa nova style?**

a. "Sweet Georgia Brown"
b. "Whispering"
c. "Stella By Starlight"
d. "The Girl from Ipanema"

**46. Which of the following reasons for administering a music aptitude test is most appropriate for use in K–12 music education?**

a. To use as tests for entrance into elite performance organizations
b. To assist in grading student achievement when compared to aptitude
c. To teach to students' individual strengths and weaknesses
d. To help students consider their choices when thinking about a career in music

**47. Which of the following techniques for determining the size of a violin or viola is most appropriate to use for beginning players?**

a. Measure from the base of the neck to the wrist, arm being diagonal to the floor and at a 45-degree angle.
b. Measure from the base of the neck to the center of the palm, arm being diagonal to the floor and at a 45-degree angle.
c. Stand and hold the instrument upright, positioning it against the left side, holding the neck with the fingers in first position where the fingers line up with the eyes.
d. Choose the right-sized chair so that there is a 90-degree angle in the legs, set the endpin around 12 inches off the ground, and the instrument should rest on the chest at a 45-degree angle with the C string peg being near the left ear.

**48. Which of the following factors related to teaching to individual differences is most evident in the rating scale illustrated below?**

**Q&A Antecedent and Consequent Phrases Improvisation Rating Scale**
1. Student responds, but the response is completely unmusical.
2. Student performs a song and a sense of melodic contour is evident. Student sings resting tone in tune. Does not demonstrate a sense of tonal syntax.
3. Student sings the resting tone and some pitches in tune, but does not sing tonal functions (e.g., V-I/IV-I or diatonic) that act as cadences in consequent phrases. Student demonstrates some sense of tonal syntax.
4. Student sings resting tone and some pitches in tune. Student sings a tonal function that can be included in a consequent phrase. Student demonstrates a sense of tonal syntax.
5. Student sings resting tone in tune and sings most tonal functions and pitches associated with a consequent phrase in tune. Student demonstrates a clear sense of tonal syntax by locking in tonality.
6. Student begins and ends in tune. Student sings all tonal functions and pitches associated with a consequent phrase in tune. Student demonstrates a clear sense of tonal syntax.

a. It is based upon the student responding with a consequent phrase.
b. It is a single-dimensional continuous rating scale.
c. The criteria within the rating scale are subjective.
d. Most students will score neither a 1 nor a 6.

**49. Which of the following modern composers, along with Phillip Glass, helped pioneer the subgenre of minimalism in music?**

a. John Cage
b. Francis Poulenc
c. Charles Ives
d. Bela Bartok

**50. When teaching a rote song, which of the following is the primary justification for the teacher using the technique of singing the song or performing an instrumental version for students while asking them to do several activities, such as raising a hand every time a specific word is sung, identifying repeating patterns, or saying what the first and last words of the song are?**

a. Promotes the creation of a gestalt during learning
b. Provides opportunities for teacher modeling
c. Efficiently and enjoyably teaches by rote
d. Students learn without realizing they are learning

**51. Which of the following harmonic analyses best represents the music excerpt below?**

(J.S. Bach chorale, BWV 26)

a. i – $V^6$ – i – i – i – VII – III – III
b. vi – III – vi – $I^{6/4}$ – vi – V – I – I
c. i – V – i – $i^6$ – vi – V – I – I
d. i – $II^{6/5}$ – $i^6$ – iv – $V^{6/4}$ – $V^7$ – vi – i

**52. Which of the following reasons for changing from a rubber to a metal mouthpiece is a general misconception among saxophone players?**

a. A rubber mouthpiece doesn't offer as much volume control.
b. A rubber mouthpiece is darker with a warmer sound.
c. A metal mouthpiece has more projection and edge.
d. A metal mouthpiece has more versatility of tone.

**53. The following music excerpt was composed by which of the following composers?**

a. Carl Orff
b. Igor Stravinsky
c. Aaron Copland
d. Dmitri Shostakovich

**54. A composer is writing a piece using the tenor clef. Which of the following instruments is she likely composing for?**

a. Viola
b. Guitar
c. Cello
d. Banjo

**55. Which of the following reasons best explains why clarinets are tuned slightly sharp by the manufacturer?**

a. Manufacturing the clarinet slightly sharp helps players perform all the tones throughout the register more closely to well-tempered tuning.
b. If a clarinet naturally plays flat with all joints pushed in, there is no easy remedy to put the instrument in tune.
c. Because there are options for purchasing shorter barrels based upon the manufacturer's design.
d. Performing slightly sharp is less abrasive on the listener's ear than performing flat.

**56. Which of the following ideas related to evidence-centered design (ECD) is the core reason for its use?**

a. Develop assessments that show competency of intended knowledge and skills.
b. Create meaningful learning experiences that transfer to real-life scenarios.
c. Design goals and measurable objectives before learning experiences.
d. Generate ideas for teachers to use when introducing new concepts.

**57. Given that the following music excerpt is a Brahms piano sonata and the excerpt begins with a time signature of 2/4 and a tempo of approximately 76 beats per minute for the eighth note, how should the 4/16 and 3/16 measures best be conducted?**

(Brahms, *Piano Sonata No. 1*, C major, Op. 1)

a. Two-pattern with eighth notes as the beat
b. Four-pattern with 16th notes as the beat
c. Two, then three-pattern with eighth notes as the beat
d. Four, then three-pattern with 16th notes as the beat

**58. What is the lower limit for a middle school male whose voice has already changed?**

a. G3
b. F3
c. A3
d. D3

**59. Which of the following regions of the world do raags come from?**

a. Australia
b. Japan
c. Africa
d. India

**60. Which music symbols, when accompanied by a note, indicates a lower mordent?**

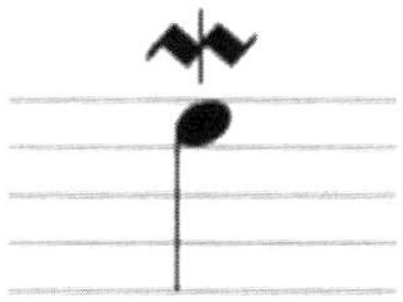

a.

b.

c.

d.

**61. Which of the following harmonic analyses best represents the music excerpt below?**

(J.S. Bach chorale, BWV 288)

a. i – $iv^{6/4}$ – $i^{6}$ – $vii^{ø7}$ – iv – $ii^{6/5}$ – V – i
b. V – $i^{6}$ – $ii^{o6}$ – $V^{4/2}$ – $i^{6}$ – $iv^{6}$ – V – i
c. i – $II^{6/5}$ – $i^{6}$ – iv – $V^{6/4}$ – $V^{7}$ – vi – i
d. III – i – V – VI – ii – V/V – i – i

**62. Which of the following reasons for having transposing instruments is best used when first teaching beginning composition and arrangement techniques to a high school clarinet student?**

a. Even though the note would sound different, it is easier for clarinetists to use the same fingerings for a written note on the entire family of different sized clarinets.
b. If there were only concert C clarinets, performing some clarinet music would not be possible because concert-pitched instruments do not easily cover the range of all clarinet solos.
c. Playing only concert-pitched clarinets (soprano and bass) would be more difficult because many clarinet parts would be in keys requiring extensive and awkward use of barrel keys.
d. Performed notes within overlapping ranges in the clarinet family that are transposing instruments sound exactly the same as written in notation.

**63. Which of the following musical terms most closely means "to become more slow and broad"?**

a. Allargando
b. Allegrezza
c. Andante
d. Assai

**64. From which of the following countries does the mbira (finger piano) originate?**

a. Zimbabwe
b. Japan
c. Peru
d. Chile

**65. Which of the following conducting patterns best fits the music excerpt?**

(Elgar Enigma Variations VII Op. 36)

a. 

b. 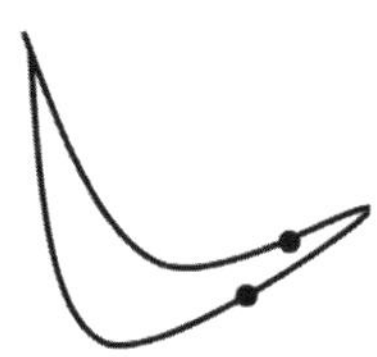

c. 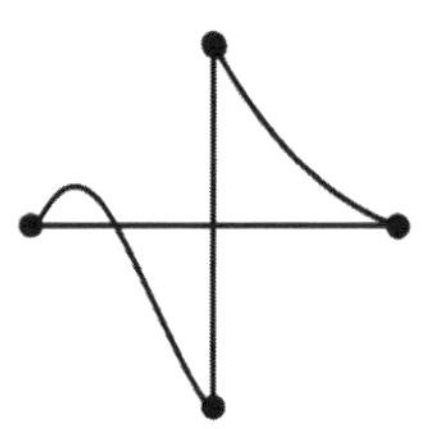

d. 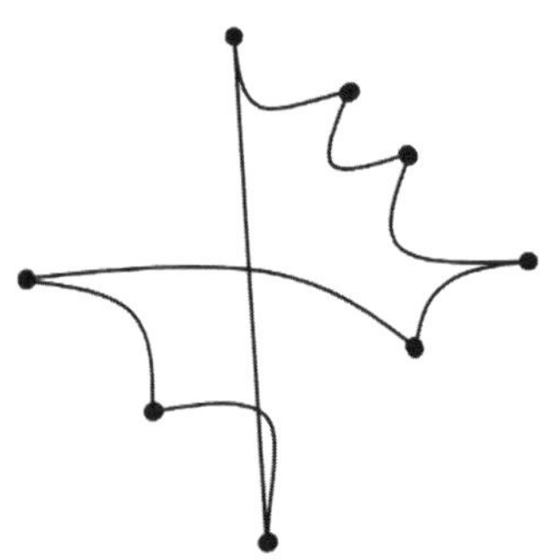

**66. For music students, which of the following movement sequences should the Laban effort elements initially be taught with?**

a. Space, weight, time, flow
b. Weight, time, space, flow
c. Time, flow, space, weight
d. Flow, space, weight, time

**67. Which of the following tonalities is the melody below composed in?**

a. Harmonic minor
b. Melodic minor
c. Phrygian
d. Dorian

**68. Which of the following bowing techniques is best characterized by strokes being played alternately up and down without the bow being lifted from the string?**

a. Martelé
b. Pizzicato
c. Détaché
d. Sul tasto

**69. Which of the following music notation copying scenarios is allowed by the 1976 Copyright Act?**

a. The teacher copies one chapter from a music theory book for students.
b. The teacher makes a copy of a score to study and mark up for rehearsal.
c. The teacher copies an entire piece onto a blackboard or an interactive whiteboard.
d. The teacher simplifies a music part for a student and alters the character of the work.

**70. Which of the following is almost always bad etiquette for a classical music performer, but not always for a member of the audience?**

a. Talking during the performance
b. Leaving a cell phone on
c. Loud page turns
d. Toe tapping

**71. Which of the following cooperative learning techniques, when used in a chamber orchestra rehearsal setting, best promotes positive musical interdependence among group members?**

a. Assign students to critique their own sections' strengths and weaknesses.
b. Have each section perform all of the other sections' parts to the extent possible.
c. Task each student to keep an individual rehearsal diary, documenting how the group improves over time.
d. Teach students interpersonal conflict resolution skills in order to prevent hurting group performance quality.

**72. Which of the following differentiated instructional strategies is most practical when teaching guitar in a general music setting?**

a. Separate high achievers from low achievers.
b. Eliminate individual formative assessments.
c. Provide each student with short personal lessons.
d. Design group projects based upon mutual interests.

**73. For intermediate to advanced clarinet players, when tuning with a band or wind ensemble with concert Bb, which of the following clarinet tuning sequences is most appropriate for a clarinet player to use when tuning his or her instrument?**

a. C4, C5
b. E3, E4
c. C5, G5
d. G3, E3

**74. When a student is given a simple melody and asked to audiationally compose a more complex melody based upon the simple melody, which of the following parts of Bloom's taxonomy of thinking skills is the student most engaging in?**

a. Application
b. Analysis
c. Synthesis
d. Evaluation

**75. Which three Western music eras can best be described as the time when polyphonic music was developed and reached its peak use?**

a. Medieval, Renaissance, Baroque
b. Baroque, Classical, Romantic
c. Classical, Romantic, Impressionist
d. Impressionist, Modern, Post-modern

**76. Which of the following characteristics about 12-tone music best explains why there are no key signatures?**

a. The music is performed using equal temperament.
b. Modern music often doesn't use time signatures.
c. Matrices use numbers instead of letter names.
d. Each pitch class is of equal importance.

**77. Which of the following four uses of the 6/4 chord does the music excerpt best exemplify?**

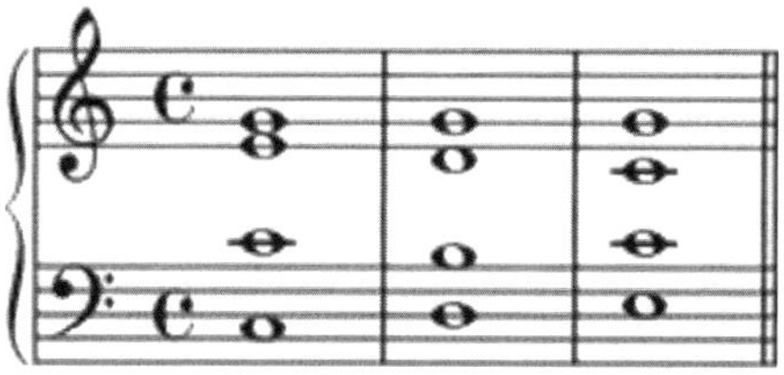

a. Cadential
b. Passing
c. Pedal
d. Arpeggiated

**78. What is the top range of flute parts in published band music that is graded level I?**

a. A5
b. C6
c. G5
d. D5

**79. Which of the following discipline principles is most related to achieving good classroom management throughout an entire school?**

a. Each classroom has a different set of rules depending upon the class and teacher's style.
b. Each teacher has an emergency clause that, when invoked, brings severe consequences.
c. Each teacher uses various disciplinary techniques depending upon the situation.
d. Each classroom has the same core classroom rules.

**80. Which of the following slide adjustments is most likely to be used when adjusting for intonation on a Bb trumpet in the last measure of the music excerpt shown below?**

a. Pull out first and third slides
b. Push in first and third slides
c. Pull out first slide
d. Push in first slide

**81. Which of the following speech, movement, and pattern sequences best represents an elementary-level Orff rhythm teaching sequence?**

a. Speech, movement
b. Unmetered speech, poetry
c. Pantomime, free movement
d. Double moving ostinatos, pitched drone

**82. Which of the following multicultural music experiences would best lead to an authentic polycultural curriculum?**

a. Students are immersed into a way of being by listening, singing, and moving to music in non-Western ways, including styles, tonalities, and meters.
b. Students research heritages of non-Western cultures, then choose to listen to songs and watch ethnological presentations about and prepare food of one of those cultures.
c. Students create a musical drama about the challenges that non-Western peoples might encounter when emigrating to the United States, then do an educational performance for the school population.
d. Students invite a non-Western music performing group to come in and sing, play, and dance for the school population and answer questions that students have as a result of their research about the culture of the invited group.

**83. Which of the following tonality sequences does Gordon advocate for as a part of learning sequence activities?**

a. Major/minor, Dorian/Mixolydian
b. Pentatonic, major
c. Mixolydian, Dorian
d. Major/Dorian, Mixolydian/minor

**84. Which pop musician directly references the excerpt of this Chopin Prelude?**

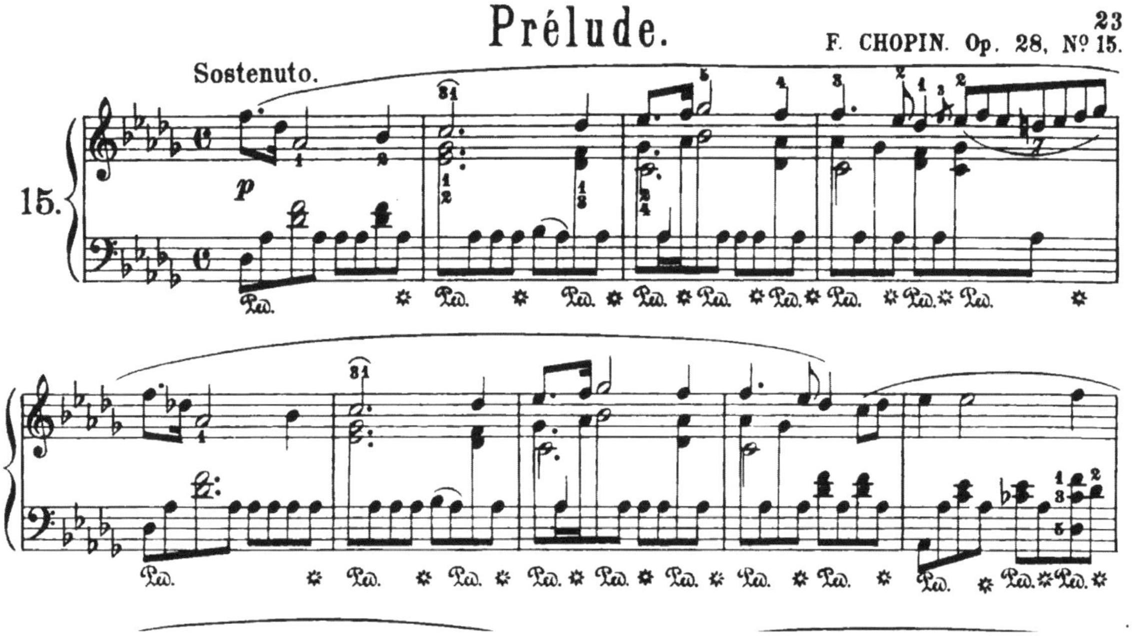


a. Stevie Wonder
b. Ray Charles
c. John Legend
d. Billy Joel

**85. How does the illustration below modify treble clef function?**

a. Raises the pitch by two octaves
b. Raises the pitch by one octave
c. Lowers the pitch by two octaves
d. Lowers the pitch by one octave

**86. The second motif of the first movement of this symphony, illustrated in the music excerpt below, begins with the cellos before moving to the upper strings. Musicians often refer to this symphony as the "symphony that ______ wrote but didn't finish." Which of the following composers wrote this symphony?**

a. Schumann
b. Berlioz
c. Schubert
d. Mahler

**87. When using a standard trigger on a Bb tenor trombone, which of the following intervals does the trigger expand the instrument's range by?**

a. Lowers by a perfect fourth
b. Lowers by a perfect fifth
c. Raises by a major third
d. Raises by a perfect fifth

**88. Which of the following instruments reads as transposed on a non-transposed score?**

a. Bass clef baritone
b. Bassoon
c. Bb tenor trombone
d. Double string bass

**89. When teaching and comparing form, genre, and subgenre, which of the following explanations is most correct?**

a. Forms are subsumed under various genres.
b. Both form and genre are largely synonymous.
c. There is a homogeneity of form within a particular genre.
d. Form represents a time period and genre represents musical structure.

**90. Which of the following musical terms most closely means "to perform gaily"?**

a. Geschwind
b. Langsam
c. Grazioso
d. Giocoso

**91. When using drones to improve intonation, which of the following sequences is most appropriate for clarinets to use in order to develop technique and audiation skill in their individual practice sessions?**

a. Tune to an octave, tune to a perfect fifth.
b. Tune to an octave, tune to a major third.
c. Tune to a perfect fifth, tune to a major third.
d. Tune to a perfect fifth, tune to a 12th overblow.

**92. Which of the following differentiated instruction strategies is the most practical technique to differentiate instruction when teaching students to audiate in an instrumental music class setting?**

a. Assigning more difficult ensemble parts to students with higher music aptitude
b. Skipping steps in Gordon's skill learning sequence when teaching students with low music aptitude
c. Teaching research-based easy, moderate, or difficult tonal and rhythm pattern content to students with varying aptitudes
d. Separating low-aptitude students from high-aptitude students when teaching learning sequence activities in order to avoid confusing low-aptitude students

**93. Which of the following trumpet ranges is most appropriately expected, as a minimum, for first-year elementary school trumpet students playing music graded level 1 (as written)?**

a. Bb3 to D5
b. C4 to C5
c. A3 to F5
d. F#3 to G5

**94. Which of the following special needs strategies most directly helps special education students who might become easily overwhelmed in the music classroom?**

a. Making sure pathways are clear and the room is very organized
b. Providing large-print music books, parts, or scores when possible
c. Modifying instruments, strikers, and bows with tape, sticky dots, and Velcro
d. Incorporating finger warm-ups and breathing exercises into instrumental lessons

**95. Why are feathered saxophone swabs taken out of the instrument during storage?**

a. They hold moisture that is wicked from the pads.
b. They bend keys when the instrument is stored in the case.
c. They become squashed when kept in the instrument.
d. They are designed to be kept in bags to keep them moist.

**96. Which of the following "Mighty Five" compositional techniques is used in the following music excerpt?**

(Rimsky-Korsakov, *Scheherazade* Op. 35, Third Movement)

a. Modular rotation
b. Russian submediant
c. Tonal mutability
d. Whole-tone scale

**97. The famous trumpet opening in this music excerpt was composed by which of the following Romantic era composers?**

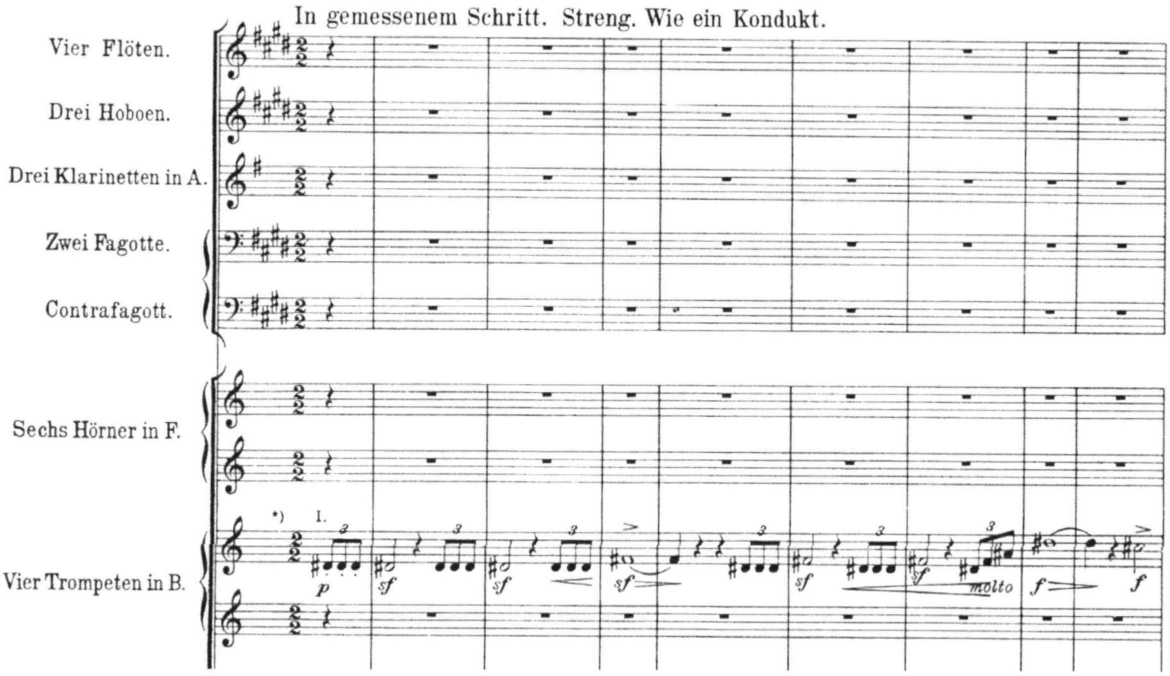


a. Mozart
b. Mahler
c. Beethoven
d. Schubert

**98. Why should trumpets be laid down with the 2nd valve slide facing up?**

a. To prevent the slide from becoming bent and stuck in place
b. To make it easier for players to move from resting to performing position
c. To distribute weight more evenly and reduce strain on the instrument's structure
d. To promote a uniform look among ensemble members when their instruments are being held at rest

**99. Which of the following parent/guardian communication techniques is the best and most inclusive way to inform these stakeholders of what is happening in the music classroom?**

a. Regular Blogs/Vlogs
b. Monthly parent newsletters
c. Classroom visits
d. Marking period summaries

**100. Which of the following practices is illegal when using music writing software that has been leased for use by one student?**

a. That student using the leased software on all of their personal computers
b. That student allowing other students to download the software for their own use
c. That student notating an original composition and printing out copies for all students
d. That student allowing his teacher to work with him while the student composes an original composition

# Answer Key and Explanations for Test #2

**1. B:** Option B is the correct answer because a large portion of what is now called classical music is sacred music. Mozart's *Requiem* is a standard part of the choral literature. It is quality literature because it has stood the test of time. It is respected by professional musicians throughout the world. It provides significant opportunities for students to improve their vocal skills, develop comprehensive musicianship, and it can be used to teach students about history and culture within an important music era. The more significant challenge for choral teachers is to be inclusive of a variety of sacred music pieces from a diversity of eras, cultures, and religions.

**2. A:** When tuning a clarinet to itself, players check intonation by comparing reference tones. The notes G4 and C5 are often used as reference tones because they represent different registers and adjustment points on the instrument. The open throat tone G4 has no fingers down, thus presenting the entire open length of the clarinet. Clarion C5 is played using both the left hand and the right hand, and the adjustment is made with the middle joint.

**3. A:** If the pitch is lower than an F#, and assuming that the barrel and mouthpiece assembly are properly in place, the student should take less mouthpiece into the mouth, firm the corners of the embouchure, blow more air, or some combination of those three techniques. If the pitch is higher than an F#, the student should take more mouthpiece into the mouth, blow less air, or some combination of those two actions. The student should practice performing on the barrel and mouthpiece when first learning to play. Performing with the correct pitch ensures that the grip, angle of the mouthpiece, amount of air used (a fast stream), and the amount of mouthpiece taken into the mouth is correct.

**4. D:** A breve is equal to a double whole note. Understanding the Latin names of notes is important when analyzing older music or transcribing for performance, for understanding notation throughout music history, and for understanding the language of music notation in Europe and conductors from around the world who still use these names.

**5. C:** This is Beethoven's famous melody from the first movement of his *Eroica Symphony No. 3* in Eb major. Shortly before composing this symphony, Beethoven went through an emotional crisis in his life, writing what has become known as the "Heiligenstadt Testament." This symphony is said to mark a change in Beethoven's writing, and it is a line of demarcation from writing in the Classical style to writing in a more Romantic style. It is characterized by a movement beyond traditional boundaries in form, length, harmony, and emotional expression.

**6. B:** Serialism is both a method and a movement. Obvious clues that this is serialistic include that the series of pitch classes are not repeated until all 12 tones are performed, the lack of a key (12-tone music treats all pitch classes with equal importance), and the presentation of all pitch classes in the first 12 tones. The title of this piece is "12-Tone Blues."

**7. C:** There are conditions of brevity, spontaneity, and cumulative effect that are typically included in fair use guidelines under the 1976 Copyright Act. Option A is incorrect because each copy must contain notice of copyright. Option B is incorrect because the limit is 250 words. Option D is incorrect because the limit is one chart, diagram, or drawing per book.

**8. A:** Guido of Arezzo (approximately AD 991 – approximately AD 1033) used this hymn, which was written to honor John the Baptist (Paul the Deacon probably wrote the words; it is unknown if Guido composed the melody) to teach a rudimentary form of solmization (the use of solfege in reading and performing music). Each phrase begins with the six syllables that Guido used in order to help singers learn chants more quickly. By recalling the chant, a singer could recall C, D, E, F, G and A (*ut*, *re*, *mi*, *fa*, *so*, and *la*). With the exception of France, *ut* was eventually replaced with *do*. The system that arose out of the Guidonian hand technique and that is the basis for teaching in the Orff and Kodály methods today (with moveable, *la*-based minor, rather than fixed-*do*) was actually developed centuries after Guido's death. Although this hymn is significant because of solmization, Guido d'Arezzo was also instrumental in developing a three- or four-line staff in which music notation could be written, replacing neumatic notation (the excerpt above is written using modern notation). Singers no longer had to rely only on memory to sing a specific chant, as neumes did not specify pitch.

**9. B:** A six-minute performance duration is reflected in the body of literature for grade level 4 works for band, and it is the suggested time length for the American Band College Music Grading Chart. It is interesting to note that grade level 4 music is shorter in duration than grade 3. This is because of the extended range and endurance required for performing without rest.

**10. A:** The use of the pentatonic scale gave the "Mighty Five" another way to sound unique compared to Western music because the pentatonic scale conveys an impression of folk music and an Eastern origin.

**11. C:** Reimer's famous book about the "feelingfulness" of music and music education became popular during the 1960s through 1980s in music education, and was later challenged by the philosophies of Edwin Gordon, who focused more on audiation. Aesthetic music education is still a cornerstone for music education and music education classes that introduce music education philosophy to future music teachers.

**12. A:** While IDEA does not define least restrictive environment (LRE), the concept includes the idea that children in special education should be included with all other children whenever possible. Options B and C are incorrect; while they are included in IDEA, they are not as explicit about mainstreaming and inclusion as LRE is. Option D is incorrect because PLP is a component of an IEP that describes current, specific, and measurable information about a student's performance that is affected by a disability.

**13. C:** Using moveable *do*, *la*-based minor (one may call it *re*-based Dorian or *so*-based Mixolydian), the tune begins on "*re*." Even though there is a raised "*fi*" in the second measure (the equivalent of an altered tone), the harmonic functions within the first section are characteristically Dorian (I IV–bVII). The second section is major sounding with a lowered seventh. The resting tone in Mixolydian is "*so*." The first note of the second section of the tune is "*ti*." The song ends on "*so*," with harmonic functions related to Mixolydian tonality outlining the second section of the tune (I–bVII).

**14. C:** Inversion is the upside-down permutation of the original tone row in 12-tone music. Prime is the original row. Retrograde is prime backwards. Retrograde inversion is prime written upside-down and backwards.

**15. D:** A synchronization (or "synch") license allows the licensee to synchronize music to visual images or recordings. A grand license is obtained for the production of large dramatic works, such as the yearly performance of a school musical. A mechanical license is obtained when someone wishes to cover a song that someone else holds copyright to. A compulsory license allows someone to cover a previously released recording of someone else's song that is copyrighted, provided royalties are paid.

**16. A:** Kodály used techniques from various music pedagogies, including Sarah Glover and John Curwen's hand signs and Émile-Jacques Dalcroze's emphasis on movement. However, he wished for all Hungarian children to become musical through the singing of folk songs of their mother country.

**17. A:** The F attachment allows a tenor trombone to play a few lower notes, but it primarily allows sixth position notes to be played in first position because it makes the instrument longer by the equivalent of five positions. Thus, instead of playing a Bb major scale with Bb = first, C = sixth, D = fourth, etc., the scale can be played Bb = first, C = first (with trigger), D = fourth, etc. This saves a lot of movement on the slide.

**18. C:** For almost all saxophone-related problems, playing just the reed/mouthpiece setup is the first step in diagnosing a problem. In the case of a middle-D not speaking, if the reed/mouthpiece setup is working, the problem is usually that the octave key mechanism is not working and may need to be bent back into position.

**19. B:** Dynamic microphones do not need a phantom power source. Although condenser microphones are more sensitive, they generally cannot handle the high sound pressure levels that dynamic microphones are made to handle.

**20. C:** Because the clarinet requires more air pressure to play (smaller aperture in the mouthpiece, smaller bore in the instrument), the embouchure must be firmer. This is accomplished by tightening the corners of the mouth.

**21. B:** The 1, 2, 3, 1, 2, 3, 4, 5 piano fingering pattern is used for the right hand C major scale. Option A is right hand Bb major scale. Option C is left hand C major scale. Option D is left hand Bb major scale.

**22. A:** The involuntary confinement of a student alone in a room in which the student is physical prevented from leaving best legally defines "physical seclusion." The difference between option A and option D should be self-evident, as emergency situations require such tactics for student safety; however, the US Department for Civil Rights has yet to address the issue of option D in its manual. Option B is incorrect because it is part of a sanctioned behavior modification program. Option C is incorrect because it is an extension of option B and is part of a timeout. The US Department Office for Civil Rights explains that restraint or seclusion should never be used as "punishment or discipline… as a means of coercion or retaliation, or as a convenience" (p.12).

**23. D:** When using a rehearsal/preparation score, the appropriate sequence for understanding a composition's form is described below in the fifth step for working with a rehearsal/preparation score for teaching and conducting.

The steps to using a rehearsal score are enumerated below.

1. Number measures.
2. If a choral piece, whisper through the text. If the text is foreign, write the literal translation down.
3. Play at the piano and sing every individual part.
4. Analyze/audiate the harmonic content.
5. Mark the form, beginning with motifs and phrases. Mark periods and cadences. Proceed to large sections. Determine form.
6. Mark expressive elements, including dynamics and dynamic terminology, articulation marks.
7. Play or finger through every part on every instrument.

8. Mark technically difficult material.
9. Create measurable learning objectives and concomitant performance rating scales.
10. Reduce the score at the piano.
11. Create an interpretation chart.
    - Where to stagger breathing
    - How to turn/shape phrases
    - Tempo/rubato/caesura
    - Music history lessons
    - Music theory lessons
    - Audiation lessons
12. Listen to the piece, preferably more than one recording. Listen last to avoid undue influence by other interpretations.

**24. A:** Backwards design begins with the end product in mind. Compared to the past, in which teachers would design activities before designing an assessment, backwards design helps teachers to structure student activities more purposely around what students are expected to know or do at the end of the learning experience. This makes backwards design the most appropriate when designing instructional content that accounts for federal, state, and professional guidelines.

**25. B:** Option B is the correct answer because standardized tests mean that all students are measured using the same material that is delivered in the same way. This provides stakeholders with reasonable access to objective data that indicates how programs, schools, and students are performing. It also is a form of mandate that steers the direction of teaching. The Iowa Tests of Musical Literacy could be used at the national or state levels for program evaluation, rather than at just the local level. Options A and C are incorrect because these are local techniques used in program evaluation. Option D is incorrect because music advocacy groups have relatively little influence at state and national levels.

**26. A:** *Sforzando* translates to "forced" and refers to a sharp accent performed on a note or chord.

**27. C:** The cajon is a wooden box percussion instrument. Peruvian slaves from West Africa created it using packing crates to replace the percussion instruments that they left behind. Western pop music has adopted the use of the cajon. Drummers can now be seen performing pop songs while sitting on a cajon and beating Western rhythm to pop music.

**28. B:** Making sure that there is a high play-to-talk ratio is relevant for both vocal and instrumental rehearsals at all grade levels. This concept ensures that students remain engaged and interested in the lessons while learning. Option A is incorrect; while it encapsulates the idea of the whole-part-whole approach to teaching, it is not a technique that should be used for every part of every rehearsal. Option C is incorrect; while sight-reading is integral to developing musicianship, it should not be considered a hard and fast rule to incorporate for every rehearsal—the needs of the moment often dictate when sight-reading can be incorporated into a rehearsal. Option D is incorrect because rehearsal pacing should generally be relatively quick. Alternating the pace between fast and slow according to the needs of the moment is a more important consideration.

**29. D:** Dynamics refer to how volume changes in a piece. In this excerpt, terraced dynamics are created by the sudden changing texture of the music. Figured bass is a defining characteristic of the Baroque era, but it is not used in this excerpt. Changing mood and balanced phrasing are more associated with the Classical era and not the Baroque.

**30. A:** The Bb side is the side that the F side is compared to, thus the Bb side is tuned first. The instrument is tuned on the Bb side to a C5 (concert F) because the horn, no matter which side is being played, is considered a horn in F, and the notation and fingerings for the concert F for each side is the same (open fingering).

After this step, one may proceed to tune each valve through a prescribed sequence of valve combinations, starting with the first valve. Note that tuning a double horn is always a compromise, and a well-developed embouchure and slight pushing in or pulling out of the hand in the bell can raise or lower the pitch.

When tuning a horn for a younger student, when tuning all of the valves, one can mark all the slides with a pencil in order to save time tuning a section the next time around.

**31. B:** The clarinet overblows at the 12th because the barrel is cylindrical and closed at one end. Option A is incorrect because saxophones are closed but conical and overblow at the octave. Option C is incorrect because the trumpet is a closed, partly cylindrical, and partly conical instrument that overblows at the octave. Option D is incorrect because a flute is an open cylinder and overblows at the octave. In other words, the saxophone, trumpet, and flute all overblow at the octave.

**32. A:** Texture is defined as layers of musical sound, and monophonic music is characterized by the performance or singing of a single melody. The melody can be performed by more than one voice, instrument, or some combination of voice and instrument. Plainchant is an excellent example of monophonic texture. Non-pitched percussion or drums in world music or Western pop music is not a consideration when thinking about musical texture.

**33. D:** The song is in major tonality and the excerpt inquired about uses the tonic and subdominant harmonic functions.

**34. C:** Part of the tonal audiation and writing subtest requires students to listen to harmonic progressions under (or over) a melody and, using chord function symbols, write the harmonic functions that they are hearing. Option D is incorrect because students are not required to improvise within the ITML.

**35. D:** The primary melody from the ballet *Polovtsian Dances* from Borodin's opera *Prince Igor* was used in the musical *Kismet* in 1953. The musical won a Tony award in 1954. The melody was used in the song titled "Stranger in Paradise."

**36. A:** This Requiem excerpt was composed by Wolfgang Mozart. Mozart was almost certainly influenced by Michael Haydn's *Requiem*. In turn, Hector Berlioz's *Dies Irae* is said to rival the magnificence of Mozart's *Requiem*. Robert Schumann proclaimed Cherubini's (a contemporary of Mozart) *Requiem* as being "without equal," and Beethoven requested that Cherubini's be played at his own funeral.

**37. A:** Students who can solfege have an easier time transposing between clefs than students who must transpose by counting up or down a whole step. Additionally, learning to read and perform from both clefs using solfege reinforces solfege skill. Option B is incorrect because that option reinforces the idea that beginning students should learn only treble clef. Option C is incorrect because it is based on the assumption that if the trumpet reads only treble clef, then the beginning baritone player should read only treble clef. Instead, the teacher should consider the comprehensive development of musicianship and the idea that learning to transpose becomes more difficult over time, rather than easier as a student gets older. Option D is incorrect because using treble clef increases the use of ledger lines as a student becomes more experienced.

Learning science informs us that:

1. Initially, learning is a process of using the concepts of same and different. Performing in two clefs produces notes that look different but sound the same.
2. When beginning students learn both clefs simultaneously and comparatively using solfege, the true confusion of transposition that occurs after a student has become used to reading only one clef is alleviated. Analogously, the student can read in two dimensions instead of one.
3. Students should be learning how to use tonal syllables (solfege) to promote audiation in general music class, particularly when taught by Orff, Kodály, and Gordon teachers. Thus, *do-re-mi*, etc. in major tonality sounds the same no matter what key it is in and how it is notated because the syntax is the same; if students know through audiation that *do-re-mi* (for example) sounds the same but looks different in various keys, they should be taught to read with solfege in various keys and tonalities (e.g., moveable *do*, *la*-based minor, or *so*-based Mixolydian).

**38. C:** The resting tone is *do* and there are two sharps in D major. The point on the alto clef shows where a C is—on the line just below the space where C is located on the treble clef. Thus, transposing down a half step places the music in the key of D. Two sharps make the excerpt D major. It becomes easier to transpose when learning to use tonal syllables (rather than intervals) when a student is audiating, particularly if that student has learned to use tonal syllables with the Kodály method or with Gordon's music learning theory.

**39. B:** A standard baritone saxophone is pitched in concert Eb. The baritone saxophone sounds an octave plus a major sixth lower than written. Modern baritones with a low A key and high F♯ key have a range from C2 to A4.

**40. A:** Weight and flow are most directly changed in this example. Laban's model related elements of bodily movement to creativity and described four continuums to taxonomize elements of motion. This was used to inspire creativity in students by having them experience paradoxical scenarios, such as "picking up a teacup filled with liquid lead." This causes the students to respond imaginatively to an unrealistic scenario. The continuums related to each of Laban's effort elements are:

| FLOW |
|---|
| Bound - - - - - - - - - - Free |
| SPACE |
| Direct - - - - - - - - - - Indirect |
| WEIGHT |
| Heavy - - - - - - - - - - Light |
| TIME |
| Slow - - - - - - - - - - Fast |

When changing the liquid in a pretend teacup from water to lead, the weight becomes heavier. This weight change makes the flow of the cup become more bound. The timing and the space are unaffected.

**41. B:** Tongue stretching exercises include sticking out the tongue in various directions as far as possible, then relaxing; yawning while producing a soft-sounding siren, which allows the tongue to come out and down; stretching the tongue out and down to produce a circle of sound that cannot be broken if the tongue is relaxed; and placing the tip of the tongue at the bottom of the front teeth and arching the tongue forward so that the back of the tongue can be felt (this exercise can also be done when placing a curl within the tongue while phonating). Options A, C, and D are all other techniques to improve vocalization by relaxing the tongue, but tongue stretches are paramount.

**42. C:** Options B and D are very popular digital audio workstations, and Option A is a popular open-source desktop music publishing application, but it is not as sophisticated as Dorico and is not the industry standard for professional music writing notation software. Ultimately, the difference in effectiveness may be dictated by features that are accessible, such as MIDI input functionality. Usually, paid software comes with more support and stronger features within the platform, however, students and teachers have access to satisfactory features through free-to-use software. For many years, *Finale* was the industry standard, but it is no longer available for sale as of 2024. Dorico has since taken a leading role in the professional space as Finale has declined.

**43. D:** While all options are important, option A is part of short-term budgeting, option B does not account for eventual capital replacement needs, and option C helps to mitigate and fund for necessary expenses. Option D, in cooperation with parent booster clubs and school administration, helps to ensure timely replacement of expensive instruments and equipment. While school budgets and fundraising can vary from school year to school year, depreciating assets and amortizing—spreading an intangible asset's cost over time (loans or rentals and leases)—helps all stakeholders to plan appropriately to replace equipment and instruments as needed. Many teachers are unfamiliar with depreciation and amortization, but there are usually parents or other stakeholders who can help with these processes.

**44. B:** Edwin Gordon's music learning theory evolved from early leaders in music education, including Suzuki, Dalcroze, and Kodály, but he has also been influenced by White, Gagné, Piaget, and Vygotsky, among others. Gordon's method primarily focused on understanding music as a whole by listening and improving auditory recognition and prediction skills, then honing in on how to perform or read music. Gordon coined the term "audiation," which refers to the internalization of music perception. Audiation plays a central role in Gordon's music learning theory.

**45. D:** "The Girl from Ipanema" is a classic performed in the bossa nova style. While percussion instruments are integral to the samba (percussion usually outnumbers other instruments), and even though the bossa nova is derived from the samba, it can be performed even without percussion. Both the samba and bossa nova can use standard "clave rhythms," which have origins in Afro-Cuban music. The bossa nova also incorporates Brazilian rhythms into its percussion section.

In Latin music, there are two general clave rhythms, where "clave" refers to the backbone of the rhythmic structure and not the actual instrument. There is the son clave (used in samba) and the rumba clave (played with the rumba). There is also something called the bossa nova clave (Brazilian clave), however, it differs from the son clave and rumba clave in that it is not a repetitive rhythm pattern that underlies a song. It is more like a motif—one may hear it within a bossa nova, but not as explicitly (remember that a bossa nova can be played even without the use of percussion instruments).

Son clave: this pattern can be played with either measure beginning the pattern (3:2 – 2:3). This is the basic pattern for Cuban son, and it is also used in samba.

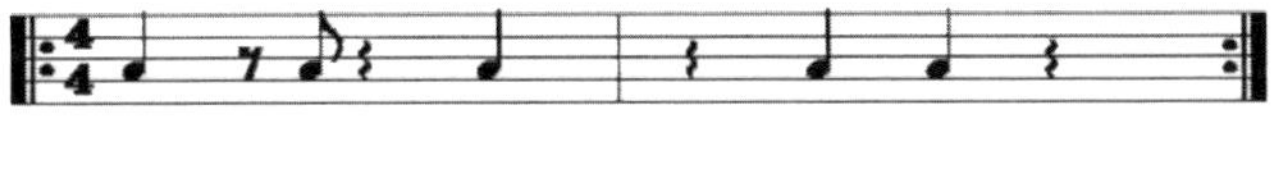

Rumba clave: this pattern can also be played with either measure beginning the pattern (3:2 – 2:3).

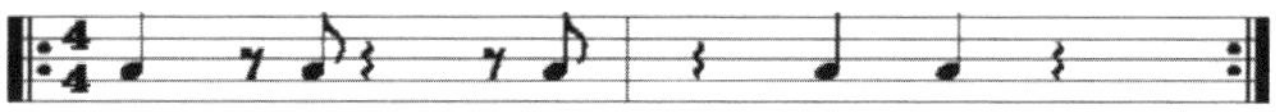

Bossa nova clave (Brazilian clave): this pattern is not a guiding pattern, but more of a rhythmic motif. Many Brazilians say that there is no clave pattern in their music and that the clave backbone is strictly Cuban.

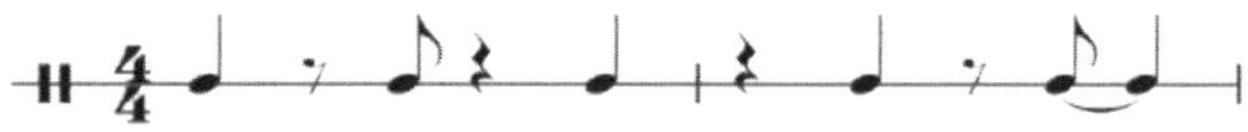

Because there are generally several percussion instruments in Latin music, there are other rhythm patterns that are imposed on these basic guiding patterns. Melodic instruments can also play additional repeated rhythm patterns under or over these basic claves and the bossa nova motif, making a polyrhythmic performance.

(Note: The late George Michael song, "Faith" (1987), contains a 3:2 son clave in the rhythm guitar. Santana's "Oye Como Va" (1970) contains another example of a son clave.)

**46. C:** Students have an inherent right to learn and be accommodated to their individual strengths and weaknesses. Options A, B, and D may all be used by teachers and students. However, because no test by itself is a perfect representation of a student's potential, along with other considerations, these options are either ancillary or ethically questionable.

**47. B:** To determine the appropriate size of a violin or viola, one should measure from the base of the neck to the center of the palm, with the arm diagonal to the floor and at a 45-degree angle. Option A is incorrect because measuring to the wrist is a popular mistake that inexperienced string teachers often make. Option C is the technique for determining the size of a double bass. Option D is for determining the size of the cello. For determining the size of the cello and bass, the size of the hand and length of the arm is also a consideration.

**48. D:** Option D is the correct answer because teachers do not want a floor or ceiling effect when working to teach to individual strengths and weakness. An arbitrary point that demonstrates minimal competency can be established at any point along the rating scale, and grades can also be arbitrarily derived along the continuum of the rating scale.

If, for example, a student scored a 6 on this ratings scale, there would be no room for that student to grow, and the teacher could not identify individual strengths and weaknesses in order to help the student improve his musicianship. Option B is incorrect because, while this is a single-dimensional rating scale, that alone does not help to teach to individual differences.

Performances that require the use of multiple rating scales (e.g., tonal, rhythmic, and expressive) can employ multiple judges in order to avoid the halo effect and so that each rating scale can be properly attended to. Or, one judge can record the performance anonymously (to avoid bias) and rate the performance for each rating scale 5-10 days apart. This takes time, but measurement and evaluation of student achievement have become high stakes. Thus, properly measuring performances is integral to the teaching and learning process and is the primary component of the teaching and learning process in evidence-centered design.

**49. A:** John Cage was also known as an experimental composer. Characteristics of minimalism include fragmented melodies; slowly changing harmonic functions; complex counterpoints, and transformations of various types (textural, dynamic, melodic and rhythmic) over a period of time.

Francis Poulenc was a French composer and pianist of the early and mid-20th century. He was influenced by Debussy, Ravel, and Stravinsky, and seemed to reject serialism for music that was "easier to listen to." His later works were influenced by his growing seriousness and religious devotion.

**50. D:** The idea that students learn by playing games and working with content and skills without explicitly being told that they are learning a particular tune or song is valuable because it makes learning fun and helps the student to learn more quickly. For example, when teaching students to learn a song at the elementary level, asking them to do four or five things, such as identify repeated rhythm patterns or words, or describe the meaning of the song, helps the student to learn the song in just a few repetitions.

Option A is incorrect because a gestalt is defined—there is no exact translation in English—as the sum being greater, or different, than the parts. Some of these techniques, such as asking students to identify the tonality or meter of a song that is being sung to them for the first time, do help to create a gestalt. But, some activities, such as remembering the first word of a song, simply help to teach the song without students being aware that they are learning it. Option B is incorrect because, while teacher modeling does help students learn the song while absorbing musical behavior, it is not the primary purpose of using this teaching technique. Option C is incorrect because, while the activity is efficient and enjoyable, the students are not always learning by rote. Rote learning is defined as learning without full understanding (e.g., students might not know the meter or tonality of the tune/song). It is usually achieved by memorization through repetition.

**51. A:** Answer choice A best represents the excerpt from Bach's chorale. BWV 26. The ability to analyze Bach chorales is integral to an understanding of music during the common practice era. When examining the bass line, remember to look for inversions, as well as keeping in mind the rules of common harmonic progressions.

**52. C:** Both teachers and students misconceive that metal mouthpieces are inherently brighter with more projection. However, many objective acoustic research studies conclude that the material that the mouthpiece is made of does not matter as much as the shape of the inside chamber in helping to create the sound. The shape of the inside chamber includes the mouthpiece tip, lay, rails, and particularly the baffle.

**53. B:** Igor Stravinsky premiered his *Le Sacre du printemps* ("*The Rite of Spring*") as a ballet and orchestral concert work on May 29th, 1913. Legend grew that the work stirred up passions to a fever pitch, causing a near riot, although this is not corroborated by contemporary reviews of the piece at the time of performance. One can identify this as *The Rite of Spring* by the above excerpt because of the driving rhythmic force of his fourths chord (Eb7 against E major), the instructions for forceful bowing, and the perceptual arhythmic nature of the excerpt through the use of accents.

**54. C:** Different clefs are used with instruments of various ranges in order to help facilitate the reading of notation. Other instruments that use the tenor clef include the bassoon, euphonium, and trombone.

**55. B:** There is one remedy for a clarinet that plays flat, and it is costly: purchasing a shorter barrel. Therefore, clarinets are typically tuned slightly sharp by the manufacturer.

**56. A:** The central reason for using evidence-centered design (ECD) is to derive a valid idea of exactly what is being measured and to ensure that artifacts and assessments used to gather evidence of proficiency or progress are measuring what they are supposed to measure. Options B, C, and D are used in ECD but are not the primary reason for its creation and use.

**57. A:** Clues as to how those measures should be conducted begin with the 2/4 measures—slow tempo with 16th note triplets moving the piece along. The rhythmic figure in the 4/16 measures is identical to a fundamental underlying rhythm pattern in 2/4, and there is no marking for a change of style or feeling of tempo. Because this is Brahms, the understanding is that the triplets in the 3/16 measures should be performed as the triplets in the 2/4 measures are performed, with the addition of more legato and with some rubato.

The entire excerpt is conducted in two, with the eighth note as the underlying feel and unifying pulse.

**58. D:** The lower limit for a middle school male whose voice has already changed is D3. Although the voice has changed, it is still developing and will not have the range—or the strength and endurance—of a choral high school tenor or bass.

**59. D:** "Raag" is another word for raga, Indian music with a melodic framework for musicians to improvise in. In American music, major and minor tonalities predominate the culture. But India has over 300 ragas, meaning "color." Just as each color is unique, each raga has a distinct sound. A raga melody is sung or played on a sitar and can be accompanied by percussion instruments, such as the tabla.

**60. A:** A lower mordent is performed by playing the principal note and the note below it very quickly before returning the principal note for the duration of that note. Option B is the Baroque era symbol for a trill. Option C is the symbol for an upper mordent. Option D is the symbol for an appoggiatura.

**61. B:** This Bach chorale is in Dorian mode, so the key signature of no sharps or flats indicates D Dorian. The first two and last two harmonic functions give clues to the correct option, as the second harmonic function is the tonic in first inversion and the second to last harmonic function is a dominant resolving to the tonic.

**62. A:** Option A is correct because transposing instruments use the same fingerings for a notated note—making it easier for a clarinetist to play on all clarinets—but, because the instruments are sized differently, they will sound differently: the larger the instrument, the lower the sound. This is the easiest and most clear explanation among the options. Option B is incorrect because, while true, it is a more detailed explanation and requires further explanation, even with examples (e.g., Mozart's *Clarinet Concerto*, K622) to clarify the point. Option C is incorrect because, while true, it may require explanation of the circle of fifths and how more sharps require more barrel keys. Additionally, the student would need to know many scales in order to concretely understand the explanation. Option D is incorrect because transposing instruments sound the same but look different in notation when a clarinetist plays the same concert-pitch note on different clarinets.

**63. A:** *Allargando* means to become more slow and broad. *Allegrezza* means cheery, joyful. *Andante* means to take at a walking pace. *Assai* means "very much."

**64. A:** The mbira originates from Zimbabwe. The mbira is a wooden box with strips of metal attached in a way that the player can pluck them with their fingers to produce different notes. The mbira has also been used by the US band Earth, Wind & Fire.

**65. B:** Elgar (1857-1934) was an English composer who wrote *Enigma Variations* in 1899. The above excerpt is from variation seven and the tempo is *presto*. Because of the phrasing characteristics, one may be tempted to conduct the piece in 4/4 like Option C, however, the tempo of the music moves so that the appropriate pattern is a two-beat pattern. The music is not quite fast enough to warrant a one-beat pattern.

**66.** D: Movement instruction, according to Laban and others, should always begin with flow. Gordon advocated beginning with non-locomotor continuous fluid motion in order to promote audiation. When music students rush a tempo, they are displacing their weight through time and space. Planning and moving over an extended period of time improves a student's sense of timing, rhythm, and expression. An excellent experience for elementary music students is to sing the song made famous by Peggy Lee, composed by Arthur Hamilton, titled *The Rainbow Song*. Students can raise their arms above their heads, holding a colored scarf in each hand, and move their arms side to side, striving to reach the end point of each side at exactly the end of each phrase of the song.

**67. C:** The resting tone in Phrygian tonality is "*mi*." Characteristic harmonic functions are i (*mi-so-ti*) – II (*fa-la-do*) – vii (*re-fa la*).

**68. C:** Détaché is a bow stroke characterized by strokes being played alternately up and down without the bow being lifted from the string. Martelé means a hammered bow stroke. Pizzicato means to pluck the strings. Sul tasto directs the player to bow over the finger board.

**69. C:** Under the 1976 Copyright Act, teachers are allowed to copy an entire piece onto a board in a classroom. Option A is incorrect because a teacher may make only one copy of one chapter from a book for scholarly research or teacher preparation. Option B is incorrect because copyright law does not allow an entire music score to be copied. Option D is incorrect because the fundamental character of the work is altered, which is prohibited by copyright law.

**70. D:** Student performers should move to the music and can gently sway during classical concerts, but toe tapping is always distracting to at least some of the audience. An audience member may quietly tap a toe if it is not distracting to others. One might think that option C pertains only to the performer, but many persons who attend concerts bring books and magazines.

**71. B:** Option B is correct; when each section learns the other sections' parts, they are made more sensitive to listening and adjusting their performance based upon what they hear when playing together. Options A and C are not cooperative learning techniques that lead to positive interdependence. Option D is a cooperative learning technique, but it is geared more toward social interaction rather than musical interdependence.

**72. D:** Option D is the correct answer because teachers can group by student preferences when offering choices of tunes or songs that students want to learn, such as learning about the history and use of the guitar in different cultural settings or genres and then having the different groups of students present their findings and perform to the rest of the class. Option A is incorrect because high and low achievers can both learn from one another (often more than they do from the teacher), even when differentiating instruction, such as progressing with tonal and rhythm patterns through Gordon's skill learning sequence, or when assigning students different tunes or songs to learn as homework in order to play for the class. Option B is incorrect because formative assessment assists the teacher in deciding how to differentiate instruction based upon achievement and preferences. Option C is incorrect because it is impractical to provide individual lessons to each student. A better option is to pair high achievers with low achievers for peer coaching.

**73. A:** The clarinet, when tuned to C4, is tuned with the barrel and first joint assembly. This joint affects not only the left-hand part of the clarinet, but also the tuning of the entire clarinet more than the middle joint and the bell joint, which are used to help tune the right-hand part of the clarinet. One tunes with the barrel and works their way down, understanding that there will always be some compromise among notes and between the top and bottom part of the clarinet. After tuning to the C4, players should tune to the C5—this tone has a natural tendency to play a little sharp. Pulling the middle joint can be used to place this tone in tune.

The significant point is to tune the left-hand first in a relatively in-tune part of the clarinet, then tune the right-hand in a relatively in-tune part of the clarinet.

When tuning to a concert A in an orchestra, some clarinet players prefer to tune to an F#4, then a B4. Another variation using the left hand is that some clarinet players prefer to start tuning with the open G4 instead of the C4, although the G4 usually has a natural tendency to play a little sharp.

The bell is used for right-hand pinky tones only.

**74. C:** Synthesis is about building a structure or pattern from diverse elements, or putting parts together to form a whole, with emphasis on creating a new meaning or structure. Both analysis and synthesis are part of Gordon's generalization level of learning within music (teaching one's self the unfamiliar based upon the familiar—unfamiliar tonalities, meters, and harmonic functions). Option A is incorrect; while it is subsumed within synthesis, it uses more familiar material. For example, one might be learning about a particular use of a second inversion tonic chord and then apply that to a composition that one is writing. Option B is incorrect because analysis uses external stimuli as the basis for thinking, and synthesis is about internal creation. An example of analysis is breaking down a score into its constituent parts in order to audiate its tonalities, meters, simple and complex motifs, phrase structures, etc. Option D is incorrect because evaluation requires making judgments about the value of ideas or materials (it's not about fit or not fit, but more about good or bad, or prefer or not prefer). As one uses higher and more complex levels of Bloom's taxonomy, one sees that the higher levels subsume the lower levels.

**75. A:** Polyphonic music in the West is known to have primarily begun developing with melismatic organum during the Middle Ages, in which an ornate musical line was added above plainchant. Polyphony further developed during the Renaissance. Motets during the Renaissance developed to be more imitative than Medieval motets. During the Baroque period, polyphony became extremely complex and reached its apex of popularity. Options B, C, and D are incorrect because, although each music era contains polyphonic music, polyphonic music was primarily developed and reached its peak use during the Medieval, Renaissance, and Baroque eras.

**76. D:** Because each pitch class is of equal importance, there is no key that 12-tone music is performed in. This style of music cannot be classified as having a tonality or even a pitch center. Each composition has its own musical syntax that cannot be generalized to another composition, such as when hearing a song in major tonality. Because each note is of equal importance, just intonation is not used. Equal temperament is used, forming an equal distance between and among notes.

**77. B:** In the passing 6/4, there is always a stepwise bass line; all voices usually move without leaps; the bass is almost always doubled; and the chord usually falls between its root position and first inversion, although it can also connect two very similar chords (e.g., supertonic and subdominant). A passing 6/4 chord moves from one related chord to another, connecting the outer chords with meaning related to the common practice period rules for composition. It can be defined by its characteristics as described above.

It is supposed to fall on the "weak" beat. However, "weak" and "strong" beats should be clarified.

For audiators, there is a difference between an accent and stress. One is in the mind (stress) and the other is performed (accent). How musical is it to accent the downbeat of every measure? Although most music students are taught that the strong beats are accented in performance, music (rhythms) flows like a river. One hears meter by grouping twos, threes, and combinations of twos and threes together in the mind (stress), not in the accenting of strong beats over weak beats in performance. One performs musically by accenting upbeats and by other means of turning a phrase. Thus, it is more accurate to say that the passing 6/4 falls on a beat which is non-stressed in audiation.

**78. B:** In published band music that is graded level I, C6 is the top range of flute parts. Some beginning flute players, particularly audiators, can use their right-hand pinky finger to perform down to a low C4 and even up to a high G6. Students who use multiple methods, one being a method that teaches audiation (e.g., *Jump Right In: The Instrumental Series*) and the other being a standard lesson book, actually tend to move more quickly through the lesson book, particularly if they are students who have at least average music aptitude. Students with low music aptitude move more slowly through the audiation-based method book and, hence, also through the standard lesson book. To be clear, achievement in audiation and in playing songs by rote and by ear in multiple keys and tonalities drive the executive (technical) skills required to move through standard lesson books. State and local performance standards reflect or are a reflection of published instrument and vocal ranges for every instrument and voice type. In establishing minimum standards, a maximum standard for most students is also established, thus protecting players from bad performance habits or physical harm by extending a range beyond what is physically reasonable.

**79. D:** At the heart of a discipline (teaching) program should be a small number of core rules that every classroom shares. This ensures that students know what to expect consistently throughout the day. While there may also be an "emergency clause" that can be invoked in exigent circumstances, that is not the glue that provides the needed cohesive structure for student expectations throughout the school.

**80. C:** The written E is usually slightly sharp, particularly in the key of C, as shown in the question. Pulling a slide out lowers the pitch and pushing the slide in raises the pitch. Because the standard fingering of the E is first and second valves, there is no need to pull the third valve slide because there is no air going through that tubing and the pitch will not be affected. Additionally, the second valve slide on a trumpet does not have a mechanism allowing it to be pushed in or pulled out during performance (it is too small). Thus, the first valve slide is used solely to adjust the pitch.

The E shown in the first measure goes by too quickly for a player to typically need to adjust, as there is no time to do so and the note goes by too fast for there to be a noticeable problem with intonation.

**81. B:** Unmetered speech precedes metered speech. Option A is incorrect because both speech and movement—broad conceptual concepts within a sequence—should be taught simultaneously. Option C is incorrect because unstructured movement precedes themed or structured movement. Option D is incorrect because performing double-moving ostinatos is more difficult than performing simple pitched drones.

**82. A:** Option A is the correct answer because the ability to hear and understand the sameness and difference and then sing and move using music elements such as meter, tonality, intonation (e.g., how Western-tuned pianos perform in Hungarian minor compared to authentically tuned indigenous instruments and voices), and styles of various cultures is the basis for authentic polycultural music education. This is a strong justification for the amount of time that music teachers should spend immersing and enculturating students to polycultural music during every music class meeting. The brain rewires itself to audiate the intonation of tonalities and meters of various cultures, just as the "L" and "R"—sounds that are not in the Japanese language—must be wired into the brain of persons who are Japanese and learning to speak English. This comes about by immersing young children in the language or music and sustaining that over an extended period of time as they change their way of being. Think of how much and how long infants listen to their mother tongue before beginning to speak it. Polycultural music education must be an integral part of every music education class in order for it to be truly polycultural music education.

**83. A:** Gordon understood that comparison by sameness and difference is the fundamental basis for all learning. Students begin with tonal patterns in major and harmonic minor tonalities not because they are inherently easier than other tonalities, but because they are the dominant tonalities in Western culture. The sequence of tonalities when using tonal patterns in learning sequence activities moves to Dorian/Mixolydian, Lydian, Phrygian, Aeolian, and Locrian while always bridging to multikeyal, multitonal, polykeyal and polytonal patterns. (Note that this does not include tunes and songs used during classroom activities—Gordon advocated using as many tonalities and meters as possible during classroom activities.) Option B is incorrect because Gordon believed that pentatonic without a clear reference to a resting tone does not promote audition—students can use any or none of the tones within pentatony as a pitch center. This does not establish an objective tonality. Thus, it does not establish a basis for sameness and difference.

**84. D:** Billy Joel directly quotes from Chopin's Op. 28, No. 15 in Db major ("Raindrop") in his introduction to the song "Souvenir" on the ninth track of his album titled *Streetlife Serenade.*

**85. D:** It lowers the pitch by one octave. One can also place a "15" below the clef to lower the pitch by two octaves. Similarly, one may raise the clef by one or two octaves by placing an "8" or a "15" above the clef.

**86. C:** This is Schubert's *Symphony No. 8*, D759 in B minor. Schubert is often regarded as a link between the Classical and Romantic eras. Schumann wrote four Romantic symphonies. The French composer Hector Berlioz wrote four Romantic symphonies, his most famous being *Symphonie fantastique*. Mahler wrote ten symphonies, characterizing the height of the Romantic era.

**87. A:** Depressing the trigger opens up additional tubing. The principle is that the bigger the instrument, the lower the sound. When using the trigger, the lowest fundamental pitch on the instrument goes from Bb to F.

**88. D:** String bass is written an octave higher than it sounds in order to make it easier to read the notation. The other options sound as written.

**89. A:** The subtleness in differences between the definitions of form and genre often creates confusion. For example, the gavotte falls within the genre of dance and the subgenre of what is now called the dance music of the Baroque era in classical music (classical music, like rock music or jazz music, might be called a type of music, a level above genre). The gavotte of the Baroque era has a particular form and style. It is a regal dance with a moderate tempo in duple meter. It is in binary form and is characterized stylistically by its homophonic texture, but especially by its relatively easy rhythms.

Similarly, the bourée also falls within the genre of dance and the subgenre of the dance music of the Baroque era in classical music. It has a particular form and style, being relatively quick, in duple meter and with homophonic texture, creating a light and lively feeling.

**90. D:** *Giocoso* most closely means "to perform gaily." *Geschwind* is German for "quickly." *Langsam* is German for "slowly." *Grazioso* means "graceful."

**91. A:** Octaves, and then perfect fifths, are among the first tones within an instrument's overtone series for students to learn. Option D is incorrect because, although the clarinet overblows at the 12th, the overblow is one of the more complex tones in the instrument's overtone series. All instrumentalists should practice drones starting with the octave and the perfect fifth.

**92. C:** Gordon objectively derived a taxonomy of tonal and rhythm patterns that helps students achieve and learn to audiate while accommodating individual differences in aptitudes. For example, when teaching a tonic function, students with low tonal music aptitude begin with easy tonic function tonal patterns, students with average tonal music aptitude begin with moderately difficult tonic function tonal patterns, and students with high tonal music aptitude begin with difficult tonic function tonal patterns. Option A is incorrect because assigning more difficult ensemble parts usually is more related to technical proficiency on an instrument, rather than individual differences in music aptitudes. It is, as Gordon said, "teaching to parts rather than teaching to music aptitudes." Option B is incorrect because no step in the skill sequence should be skipped if the goal is efficient learning. Option D is incorrect because students of various aptitudes learn from each other at least as much (if not more so) than they do from the teacher.

**93. A:** In general, first-year elementary trumpet students playing music graded level 1 should be expected to play in the Bb3 to D5 range. There is, of course, variation among students. Those who are taught to audiate tend to have a larger range—the range follows the ear rather than the other way around.

**94. A:** Some students get easily overwhelmed if a music classroom is cluttered. Options B, C, and D are accommodations and modifications that can be made for children with special needs, but they are not specific to helping a student who might become easily overwhelmed in the music classroom. Option D may be used, in particular, when a child has occupational therapy.

**95. A:** Although some feathered swabs have caps and look as though they should be stored in the saxophone during storage, and they are quite fashionable to many students, they are meant to take the moisture out of the instrument after playing so that the pads do not become ruined. Since the swabs hold moisture, they should be removed from the saxophone during storage so that damp material is not left against the pads.

**96. B:** The Russian submediant was used by the "Mighty Five" to help give a characteristic Russian sound, from village songs to church hymns and Cossack dances. It is characterized in music in major tonality by the harmonic progression that includes the major tonic—augmented tonic—minor submediant in first inversion. This can be heard in measures four and five from Korsakov's excerpt above.

**97. B:** This is the famous opening ("Marche Funebre") to Mahler's *Symphony No. 5* in C# minor. Gustav Mahler (1860-1911) is probably best known for bringing the symphonic form to its apotheosis during the Romantic era. He composed nine symphonies, with *No. 5* arguably being his most famous. His late Romantic style is evidenced by the length, song-like melodic structure, complex harmony, and overall dramatic nature. His symphonies are among the most performed even to this day. The excerpt above is a standard literature for trumpeters auditioning for any major modern symphony orchestra.

**98. A**: The 2nd valve slide is among the most vulnerable parts of a trumpet. Pressure or accidental dropping of the instrument often causes this valve slide to be bent and stuck in place.

**99. A:** While invitations to parents to visit the classroom on a regular basis are important opportunities for parents to see what is happening in the music program, many parents cannot take time out of their day to regularly come to visit the classroom. Emailing blogs with videos of students engaged in classroom activities allows parents and other stakeholders to see and hear what is happening in the classroom when they do not have the time to physically attend classes. Weekly newsletters and marking period summaries are also important tools for communicating and gaining stakeholder buy-in, but are not as personal, informative or complete as regular blogging/vlogging.

**100. B:** Persons who sign an agreement with a company to lease a single user license cannot share that software with others. Usually, a license will allow a set number of devices to install the software on, but the license may still have stipulations that only one user may make use of the software.